breathe
Think
LEAD

LESSONS FOR LEADERS
BY TED FEDERICI

Ted Federici
31 Cedar Street
Center Moriches, NY 11934
tedfederici@federicicoaching.com
www.federicicoaching.com

Breathe, Think, Lead
Lessons for Leaders

This collection of essays is dedicated to Rob Berkley, Deb Phillips, Laura Federici, and Roger Getty without whom it would not have been written. Thanks to Glen Nelson for editing this book, and DEBorahROBINSON for the book jacket design.

Table of Contents

FOREWORD

by Adam Ginsburg

No matter their field, successful business professionals typically end up devoting more time and attention on managing their organizations and less on the particular skills or talents that brought them success to begin with. Achieving success at the executive level, therefore, requires leadership skills that are distinct from parochial business issues. Through my conversations and coaching sessions with Ted Federici over many years, I have learned that it is possible to hone the tools necessary to be an effective leader. With this collection of accessible and insightful essays, Federici lights the path to help any executive find the right approach to effectively address leadership issues.

Breath, Think, Lead is not a how-to book. Mr. Federici's primary goal is not to provide step-by-step instructions for becoming a proficient leader. Instead, he offers a more universally useful approach that, taken as a whole, teaches its readers how to think like leaders. These essays do include immediately useful gems of business wisdom, but the deeper value of this book is realized through the clarity it will bring to its readers who apply the levelheaded philosophy it contains to their own situation.

I keep Ted's book on my nightstand so I can spend a few minutes reading a random essay here or there. It reminds me of things I forgot or should have known, grounds my thinking, and most importantly, helps me to Breath, Think (and) Lead.

Adam Ginsburg, Co-chairman
GDC Properties, LLC

INTRODUCTION

It's About Change!

This collection of essays is designed to get one thinking and to push the understanding that if we do not change and grow, we become irrelevant. Irrelevant as people or as a business.

Most people have had a number of careers: one or two they may have liked and prospered in. Some they did one or the other, and unfortunately, some in which they did neither.

Those of you who have achieved in at least one career all you had hoped and dreamed of in terms of financial rewards and recognition know what I mean. However, personal growth, contribution to the world in which we live and self-fulfillment may have been put on hold.

We all know, however, that financial success can take its toll. Health issues, personality change, stressed relationships, and perhaps the worst of all, the feeling of not having fulfilled one's personal creative potential.

There comes a time when one is entitled, yes that is the right word, to choose what the next phase of one's life will be.

This special time in your life can come because you have achieved all you set out to do financially; but don't know how to get out of the present. Or, fear that the enterprise you leave behind will fail with out you. And, even fear that the business defines you: read as you won't know what to do every day!

Other reasons may be that you are burned out, have been asked to leave. Perhaps, you and your partner's goals are no longer aligned. Perhaps you have become ill and cannot do what you did before and it is simply time to plan an orderly management succession.

The magic here is that you have the financial ability to make new choices!

This thinking and what I propose later on may not be right for those who are still upwardly mobile and are yet to achieve their greatest financial or personal goals. The rub is however; these rewards often come after leaving what you thought was your best vehicle for success.

Let's imagine for a moment that you are one who is defined by your work and believe that is who you are. You may also believe that there is really nothing else for you to do in life. Or, nothing you want to do.

Do you enjoy being Mr. or Ms. In-charge? Do you enjoy the prestige of recognition by your employees and or your peers in your industry? But suppose you have topped out and the business needs a new leader. Or, suppose you are asked to leave. Or how about, you know you are topped out and want to leave. How about, it is simply time to do something that you want to do!

Hard to give up all that may define your work life and often-personal life as well? I agree.

I will share my personal story with you since I think it will shed light on the process one can use to make change that replaces all you now think defines you.

I am one who was tapped out, burned out and no longer enjoyed the responsibilities I had.

I began my working career with the Bell System after college. I stayed with the system for 33 years because it offered me work I truly enjoyed. It offered as well financial and social stability, pension and health care at retirement and a network of people who would be my life long friends.

There came a time, however, when I realized that I had achieved all I had hoped for with the Bell System (Officer Level) and that I knew little of the rest of the world.

I had travelled extensively worldwide for pleasure and business; yet thought there must be more personal growth, financial gain or just plain excitement I could find.

It took me three months to mentally get to a place where I could courageously make a decision. So, after much thought, consultation, and sleepless nights, I found the courage to retire. I do not exaggerate when I say courage.

I also changed everything I could about me within reason: grew a beard, moved to Florence, Italy, rented an apartment, enrolled in both language and cooking schools. In short, I enjoyed myself (interesting choice of words even now) because I had freedom to do what pleased and enriched me.

I also began practicing yoga, reading spiritual material, and under-standing what a spiritual journey is about.

During that year, a friend became president of a major, national not-for-profit. She decided, along with the Board, that a major reinvention, restructure and new mission were required for the foundation.

She asked if I would join in this effort and take on the job of COO. I agreed to do so since "pay back" was much in order in my life.

You see, having had the courage to change my life had reenergized me completely and allowed me take on new challenges.

After a thorough review of the foundation, we decided that a five year plan was to be executed after which I would be free to move on and she could pick a "kinder more gentle" COO. I stayed five years to the day and we achieved all we set out to do.

I was completely energized by the experience; but more so by the freedom to make choices and fulfill my own potential!

During the next five years, after leaving the foundation, I became a corporate adventurer taking on jobs that interested me and used my skills. For example, I became a VP for AmeriCast in a two-year deal with a mission to marry conduit and content for television. Next, President of an American owned but Russian operated communications company, with a move to Moscow.

Upon my return to the US, I began executive coaching because over time friends and colleagues asked my help and support in operating their own businesses or changing their life's direction. I found that coaching enabled me to fulfill my Vision of my self and to make a contribution to my world. I could share all I had experienced and learned with others.

Here is the point. Along the way, I found that it took courage to invent my self every day, to write a Vision for my self and then continuously measure my life decisions against it.

As a coach these last 13 years, I have helped accomplished people to change their lives. Some were asked to leave their businesses; others wished to turn the leadership over to younger executives to ensure the firm's long-term success and still others who were no longer fulfilled. Out of these experiences I created a process to take accomplished, successful people to a new Vision and a new life.

I have taken fear out of the decision to change. I have replaced fear with positive action that we all recognize makes change possible, positive and effective.

The process starts with a personal acknowledgement that a new choice is in order. The acknowledgment comes during a personally designed Clarity Day.

Next, is the work of writing the Vision statement that will guide you for the rest of your life.

The follow-on work occurs over a planning period in which individual coaching sessions create the strategies, tactics and plan for a next phase of life.

As you know well, execution of any plan is the key to success and it is that work that creates change.

So, time to make change? Time to reinvent yourself? Time to take fear out of the equation and replace it with positive action?

These ideas are gleaned from personal executive experience, articles and books by my favorite social scientists such as Peter Drucker and BF Skinner, the internet, and absorbing many lectures, articles and seminars over the years.

Read these essays, find courage to create a new reality, and get on with it!

CHAPTER ONE:
GETTING STARTED

Love or Fear: Which Drives Your Leadership Style?

Success in leading any organization, no matter what its purpose, comes about through a conscious process that involves learning, remembering, and executing leadership techniques. This book is titled, "Breathe, Think, Lead" because we, as leaders, need a reminder to stop and regain our balance, occasionally. Every once in a while, we lose our footing. We feel overwhelmed. In such moments, I tell my clients to stop for minute: "Breathe, Think, Lead."

You probably already know most of what you need in order to be successful; you just have to remember to use what you know. If that's true, why read any further? Because the clutters of negative energy, distractions, fear, ego, and even some success in your efforts to lead can cause you to forget what you know and how to behave. So it is helpful to revisit the techniques that drive and sustain successful behavior. And leadership is all about life-long learning. No matter how seasoned a leader you are, there will be insights in these chapters that will help you recharge your leadership batteries.

There are a few surprises in the techniques for leading successfully. They make sense. You have used them yourself, and you can remember when you have been the beneficiary of the good leadership techniques of others...and when you have not. These remembered images are crucial in forming a pattern of successful leadership behavior and action. In short, these remembrances determine "who shows up for work" every day.

Let's start with two definitions to frame the discussion. In my experience, leaders manage others by using either love or fear. It seems that it should be more complex than that, but it usually boils down to those two base emotions. Which kind of leader are you? Do you rule the roost with an iron fist, or are you more likely to play to your employees' intimate and personal relationship-connected emotions? My Webster's dictionary defines love as "an unselfish loyal benevolent concern for another." Expanded for our purposes, it asks the leader to have a personal security, courage, tolerance toward, and appetite for an individual or team working toward a common goal. Such a leader helps others achieve their potential as well as striving to reach a shared vision.

Fear, on the other hand, is "a general term that implies a person's loss of courage, anticipation of danger, a painful agitation in anticipation of danger or failure." Leaders who rely on fear as a motivator sense that they may lose control, not win, not gain the rewards to which they are entitled. They may also see their individuals and teams as obstacles to their own success, and they may use any means at their disposal to subdue such a threat.

Needless to say, there are many examples of successful leaders whose style is love or fear. I'm sure you have been motivated by both impulses in your life. But again, which are you?

Few of us think we have the ability to decide who we are each day. We imagine that our personalities are set. But we do choose our behavior each day. It is our behavior that is perceived by others. We have the choice of behaving from either a basis of fear or love. Our behaviors are anything but set. We have the power within to change anything about our environment or ourselves that we do not like or that does not represent the best vision of our surroundings or ourselves.

The questions are: do we have the courage to break out of the boxes we find ourselves in, the confidence to do something differently? Do we have the courage to execute different behavior? The first step to having courage is to forgive yourself for things you did yesterday that do not represent the true you. Move on. Next, resolve to do better, to represent your best vision of yourself.

If you think about it, you can come to the conclusion that quite possibly there are only two human reactions to life's events or your behavior: love or fear. The others, such as jealousy, rage, hubris, me-first, winning, etc., derive from fear or love.

As leadership styles, fear and love are decidely different approaches with specific outcomes. Fear creates a style of leadership in which one must always be in control and openly or passively exercises ultimate decision-making. The leader who operates on the basis of fear stifles growth of people and organizations no matter how apparently successful he or she is. This leader sets the atmosphere in which no one else matters, and failure to live up to expectations (which make the leader look good) is unacceptable.

Ted Federici

Acting or reacting from fear is the chief culprit of poor leadership and unproductive behavior. It is a behavioral approach that once understood can be changed. We are not stuck with it for life. We can change. We can also learn to manage fear-driven behavior in others, once we recognize it.

Don't be afraid: it's not helping you succeed.

Mistakes

It's hard to avoid certain mistakes, especially when you face a situation for the first time. In fact, many of the following mistakes are hard to avoid even if you're an old hand. Of course, these are not the only mistakes CEOs make, but they sure are common enough.

Take the following self assessment: give yourself ten points for each of these entrepreneurial blunders you are in the process of making. Deduct five points for those you have narrowly avoided. Your score, of course, will be kept confidential, but do seek help. Fast!

1. Do you have "Big Customer Syndrome"?

Do more than 50 percent of your revenues come from any one customer? If so, you may be headed for a meltdown. While it both is easier and more profitable to deal with a small number of big customers, you become quite vulnerable when one of them contributes the lion's share of your cash flow. You tend to make silly concessions to keep their business. You make special investments to handle their special requirements. And you are so busy servicing that one big account that you fail to develop additional customers and revenue streams. Then suddenly, for one reason or another, that customer goes away, and your business borders on collapse.

Use that burgeoning account as both a cause for celebration and a danger signal. Always look for new business. And always seek to diversify your revenue sources.

2. Are you creating products in a vacuum?

You and your team have a great idea. A brilliant idea. You spend months, even years, implementing it. When you finally bring it to market, no one is interested. Unfortunately you were so in love with your idea you never took the time to find out if anyone else cared enough to pay money for it. You have built the classic better mousetrap.

Do not be a product searching for a market. Do the market research up front. Test the idea. Talk to potential customers, at least a dozen of them. Find out if anyone wants to buy it. Do this before anything else. If enough people say "yes", go ahead and build it. Better yet, sell the product at pre-release prices. Fund it in advance. If you don't get a good response, go on to the next idea.

3. Do you have equal partnerships?

Suppose you are the world's greatest salesman, but you need an operations guy to run things back at the office. Or you are a technical genius, but you need someone to find the customers. Or maybe you and a friend start the company together.

In each case, you and your new partner split the company 50/50. That seems fine and fair right now, but as your personal and professional interests diverge, it is a sure recipe for disaster. Either party's veto power can stall the growth and development of your company, and neither holds enough votes to change the situation.

Almost as bad is ownership split evenly among a larger number of partners, or worse, friends. Everyone has an equal vote and decisions are made by consensus. Or, worse still, unanimously. Yikes! No one has the final say, every little decision becomes a debate, and things bog down quickly.

To paraphrase Harry Truman, the buck has to stop somewhere. Someone has to be in charge. Make that person CEO and give them the largest ownership stake, even if it's only a little more. 51/49 works much better than 50/50. If you and your partner must have total equality, give a one percent share to an outside advisor who becomes your tie-breaker.

4. Are your prices too low?

Some entrepreneurs think they can be the low price player in their market and make huge profits on the volume. Would you work for low wages? Why do you want to sell at low prices? Remember, gross margins pay for things like marketing and product development (and great vacation trips.) Remember, low margins = no profits = no future. So the grosser the better.

Set your prices as high as your market will bear. Even if you can sell more units and generate greater dollar volume at the lower price (which is not always the case), you may not be better off. Make sure you do all the math before you decide on a low price strategy. Figure all your incremental costs. Figure in the extra stress as well. For service companies, low price is almost never a good idea. How do you decide how high?

Raise prices. Then raise them again. When customers or clients stop buying, you've gone too far.

5. Do you have enough capital?

Check your business assumptions. The norm is optimistic sales projections, too-short product development timeframes, unrealistically low expense forecasts, and underestimating competitors. Regardless of the cause, many businesses are simply undercapitalized. Even mature companies often do not have the cash reserves to weather a downturn.

Be conservative in all your projections. Make sure you have at least as much capital as you need to make it through the sales cycle, or until the next planned round of funding. Or lower your burn rate so that you do.

6. Are you out of focus?

If yours is like most companies, you have neither the time nor the people to pursue every interesting opportunity. But many entrepreneurs —hungry for cash and thinking more is always better—feel the need to seize every piece of business dangled in front of them instead of focusing on their core product, service, market and distribution channel. Spreading yourself too thin results in sub-par performance.

Concentrating your attention in a limited area leads to better-than-average results, almost always surpassing the profits generated from diversification. Al Reis, of *Positioning* fame, wrote a book that covers just this subject. It's called *Focus*.

There are so many good ideas in the world; your job is to pick only the ones which provide superior returns in your focus area. Don't spread yourself thin. Get known in your niche for the thing you do best, and do that exceedingly well.

7. Are you infrastructure crazy?

Many a startup dies an untimely death from excessive overhead. Keep your digs humble and your furniture cheap. Your management team should earn the bulk of their compensation when the profits roll in, not before.

The best entrepreneurs know how to stretch their cash and use it for key business-building processes like product development, sales and marketing. Skip that fancy phone system unless it really saves time and helps make more sales. Spend all the money really necessary to achieve your objectives. Ask the question: will there be a sufficient return on this expenditure? Everything else is overhead.

8. Do you suffer from perfectionitis?

This disease is often found in engineers who won't release products until they are absolutely perfect. Remember the 80/20 rule? Following this rule to its logical conclusion, finishing the last 20 percent of the last 20 percent could cost you more than you spent on the rest of the project. When it comes to product development, Zeno's paradox rules. Perfection is unattainable, and very costly at that.

Plus, while you're getting it right, the market is changing right out from under you. On top of that, your customers put off purchasing your existing products waiting for the next new thing to roll out your doors. The antidote? Focus on creating a market-beating product within the allotted time. Set a deadline and build a product development plan to match. Know when you have to stop development to make a delivery date. When your time's up, it's up. Release your product.

9. Do you have no clear return on investment?

Can you articulate the return that comes from purchasing your product or service? How much additional business will it generate for your customer? How much money will they save? What? You say it's too hard to quantify? There are too many intangibles? If it's too difficult for you to figure, what do you expect your prospect to do? Do the analysis. Talk to your customers. Create case studies. Come up with ways to quantify the benefits. If you can't justify the purchase, don't expect your customer will. If you can demonstrate the great return on investment your product provides, sales are a slam-dunk.

10. Are you unwilling to admit your mistakes?

Of all the entrepreneur's mistakes, this might be the biggest. At some point you realize the awful truth: you have made a mistake. Then what? Admit it quick. Redress the situation. If not, that mistake will get bigger and bigger. Sometimes this is hard, but, believe me, bankruptcy is harder.

Assume your costs are sunk. Your money is lost. There is good news:

your basis is zero. From this perspective, would you invest fresh money in this idea? If the answer is no, walk away. Change course. Whatever. But do not throw any more good money after bad. Everybody makes mistakes. Just try to catch them quickly, before they kill your company.

The Test

I have never met anyone who left his or her job (whether fired or voluntarily) who started his or her own business—and regretted it. What these people always regret is not having done it sooner. This includes people who eventually failed and had to go back to work for someone else.

Afraid to try something new? Most of us are. But our regrets will invariably be for what we didn't do rather than for what we did. So are you ready to be an entrepreneur? Do you have the right stuff? Before you take the plunge and start your own business, take this test:

Do you need a new idea?

It isn't the quality of the ideas you have that will determine whether you are successful; it's the qualities you bring to those ideas. New ideas are wonderful if you can come up with them. *But your best chance of success is working hard, using established values and ideas if necessary.*

Who are your customers?

"Everyone" is the wrong answer. If your concept is going to succeed, you have to identify a realistic target audience—big enough to be profitable yet small enough for you to service it thoroughly. Why should anyone want to buy your product or service? Find an unmet, unanswered need by identifying a market segment that isn't being served or is being served inadequately. For example, take the post office that served everybody, but unprofitably. Then FedEx and UPS jumped in and redefined the industry. They are profitable, while the post office is bleeding red ink.

Who is your competition?

If there is a market for your product or service, someone is supplying that market. He may be using another product. Or she may be using a nearly identical product that you can beat on quality, performance, or service. Either way, the existence of competition is a mixed blessing. It doesn't really matter how many others are doing something similar. All you have to do is find a way to do it better.

What advantages does your organization have over the competition?

Management? People? Product? Service? Financial strength? Reputation? Recognition? Marketing? One is not enough. Sometimes all are not enough. But you can usually beat better-financed competition with superior customer advantages.

Do you have a business plan?

If you haven't gotten around to that, make one before you do anything else. It serves several very useful purposes. It forces you to think your way through the startup process and your long-range goals. It's also a document you'll need if you plan on getting outside financing from anyone except your relatives. If it isn't persuasive and effective to an independent outside business person, that might tell you something about your real chances for success.

Your plan should include a situation analysis; objectives; target audiences; mission statement; objective; strategy and tactics; execution; budget; measurement; and time and action calendar.

What do your banker and lawyer say?

Bankers see and evaluate business plans all day long. That's their business. They might even have seen one like yours. And while you're at it, ask if they would lend you money to finance your business. Attorneys can help you avoid pitfalls. They are there to protect you.

What does your mentor say?

Find a "tiger," preferably someone who's been around the block. Retired or active professionals are a marvelous resource for this kind of advice. They also have the time, patience, skill, wisdom and understanding to help and sometimes, just to listen. They are invaluable at helping you expand your network of contacts.

Have you done an honest self-survey?

Do you really want to do this or are you just trying to escape your own problems? Be brutally honest and make sure the problem is not you. If you're going to be an entrepreneur, you have to believe in yourself more than you believe in anything else in the world.

What will you do if you fail?

Don't be discouraged if you do fail. Few entrepreneurs make it the first time they try. Failure teaches you not to fear failure because if you can survive it to fight again, you haven't failed. You have only heightened your appreciation of success.

If you're looking for a big opportunity, look for a big challenge.

The Value of Your Business

If you're like me and passionately roll up your sleeves to work on your business, you owe it to yourself to have a final result for your efforts that is truly a masterpiece.

I'm talking about your business, once it's complete...done...ready to sell for as much as you can reasonably expect, often for several times it yearly earnings. If and when it does come time to sell, you want to be selling from a position of strength—to sell it when it is at its most valuable point and not when you're burned out, in ill health, or in some other situation where you are rushed or won't make nearly as much from the sale.

Like any great work, you have to start with the end in mind, so I'll clarify just what a "sellable" business looks like. This will give you an ideal to work towards and guide your plans and work. Below are several things to be aware of in increasing the value of your business to yourself and potential acquirers.

Position your company in a clearly-defined niche. Your business must be the best it can be at what it does, without trying to be everything to everyone. A business that knows its customer segments, their needs and language, and how to solicit a response from them is a lot more valuable than one that is a mixture of everything, or an unknown in the market.

Coach your team to run the business without you. Could other people ever run your business without you? They'll have to, if you're selling! So why not make this your goal from Day One? Make an organizational chart of how your business will look when it's time to sell it. List all the various workers in marketing, operations, and those they report to. It's okay if it's just you or a handful of people currently filling all those roles. Doing this will help you organize who is going to do what in your business before you hire a new person. Then, over time, you can find other people to fill those positions one by one until you're out of the picture.

Build relationships with customers. Goodwill, such as your reputation and brand in the minds of your current and prospective customers, is considered an asset on your company's balance sheet. You build this over time by treating people right and maintaining good relationships. If you intend to sell your business someday, or if you just want to have the op-

Ted Federici

tion, this is something that you have to make a priority throughout the business's life. you can't just start doing it well suddenly in the final year. Relationships and recognition take time.

Make sure you're stable. Make sure you're not overly dependent on any one customer, vendor, employee, or anything else. Diversify your strengths. if you have any "whale" customers that make up a large portion of your business, try to get at least 80% of your business from other people. The new owner does not want to take the reins and have revenues drop in half in the event your biggest customer leaves.

Maximize your revenues. This one's self-evident, but deserves to be repeated. There are four proven ways to increase your revenues—getting more customers, increasing your average order size, get customers to buy more frequently, and finding new ways to monetize your customers and visitors. A company with higher revenues and which shows growing revenues will be more valuable and attractive to buyers.

Hold expenses accountable. You boost your net profit (and therefore the value) by reducing your expenses. However, no one ever shrank themselves into wealth. you're not going to grow your business by keeping expenses lower—but the numbers will increase as it grows. Basically, you'll want to make sure that budgets are made and followed, to keep spending within projected limits and to avoid costs creeping up that don't generate more revenue in return.

Keep great records for the next owner. Keep excellent records of everything for the new owners—your files, databases, customer communications, marketing materials, financial records, employee agreements—everything. Committing to do this now will make your life so much easier between now and the time you sell. Keep good records for your own efficiency, protection, and to make your business look a lot more attractive to buyers than one where all the records are filed away in the old owner's head.

Develop a plan for when it's "done" and ready to sell. I don't want you to have plans on top of plans, but each of these will take certain actions to make them happen. So here's what you do: Add these end results into your existing business plan, and use your best judgment when choosing how to make each of them happen in your company. When it's all said and done, the next few years are going to go by whether you maximize your business's value or not. At the end of, say, five years, would you rather have a stable, attractive, polished business ready to sell for top dollar, or be left taking what you can get for what you have? If it seems like a lot, remember you have until the time you sell to take care of these things. You don't have to do it all now! Just add these elements I described to your vision of what you want your company to be, and keep your eye on it until the big day finally comes.

Ted Federici

Start-up Capital

With the Internet making several new forms of funding available to entrepreneurs who want to sidestep the hassles and qualification of getting bank financing, there's a little confusion about peer-to-peer lending sites and how they're different from crowd funding.

Peer-to-Peer lending

Peer-to-Peer (or P2P) lending transactions occur between individuals without going through a bank or traditional intermediary. Without the middleman, borrowers can get better terms and access to more capital than before, and lenders can earn higher returns.

As can be expected, there are several popular websites that connect borrowers and lenders directly, such as: Prosper.com, LendingClub.com, Zopa.com, and IOUCentral.com.

The downside of P2P lending is that supposedly less than 10% of loans applied for on these sites get funded. And you have to pay back the loans.

Crowd funding

With crowd funding, you can tap a lot more investors and raise unlimited amounts of money. You provide rewards for those who give you money rather than needing to repay a loan, and your chances of raising crowd funding are much higher than with P2P lending. Statistics show that 50% of entrepreneurs who try to raise crowd funding successfully do so.

Regarding rewards, with crowd funding you want to offer *something* to the people who help fund your project, such as future redemption of the product or service you are creating, discounts, prizes, gifts, and bonuses. A percentage of the money raised will, in all likelihood, come from friends, family, and people in your existing contacts. However, crowd funding sites give you an organized and safe way to advertise the opportunity, and people can see the social proof of others getting on board and funding your project.

Examples of crowd funding sites are: Kickstarter.com, Rockethub.com, IndieGogo.com.

There is also a type of funding called "Micro-funding," which is a means of offering funds to impoverished people who don't have access to traditional forms of loans. These funding amounts are generally very small and are used by the recipients to launch personal businesses, such as sewing, trading, making crafts, and other manageable ventures where a little funding can go a long way for the person and their family.

I prefer crowd funding over Peer-to-Peer lending because of the potential to raise more money through a larger group of people, and not having to pay the money back (nor interest). However, I like diversifying my funding, so you should also check out the P2P lending sites to decide if they're worth pursuing for your business.

Raising Money:
What Not to Say and What Not to Believe

These days, several of my clients are writing a business case and/or an investment memorandum hoping to attract investors. As I have written before, the VC (venture capitalist) is an expensive, hard to crack route, and for smaller businesses (today) or amounts, I am recommending "angel investors." That is, people you may know who have the capability to invest and would be attracted by both your idea/product, and a interest rate that exceeds anything available in the market.

Read these two sets of top ten lies: one of entrepreneurs and one of investors, so that you know what not to say and what not to believe.

Top Ten Lies of Entrepreneurs
1. "Our projections are conservative."
2. "Jupiter says our market will be $50 billion in ten years."
3. "Several Fortune 500 companies are set to do business with us."
4. "No one else can do what we're doing."
5. "Hurry up because other investors are about to do our deal."
6. "Our product will go viral."
7. "The large companies in our market are too big, dumb, and slow to compete with us."
8. "Our management team is proven."
9. "We filed patents so our intellectual property is protected."
10. "All we have to do is get 1% of the market."

Top Ten Lies of Investors
1. "I liked your company, but my partners didn't."
2. "We are patient investors who want to help you build a great company."
3. "If you get a lead, we'll invest too."
4. "There are no companies in our portfolio that conflict with what you're doing."
5. "Show us some traction, and we'll invest."
6. "We love to co-invest with other firms."
7. "We're investing in your team."
8. "We have lots of bandwidth to dedicate to your company."

9. "This is a plain, vanilla term sheet."
10. "We will get other companies in our portfolio to work with you."

Do you know what the difference is between the lies of entrepreneurs and the lies of investors? *The investors have money.*

It's not all bad news. Think of everything that an entrepreneur needs (tech ones, anyway), and you'll see that most things are free or cheap.

As Jeff Jarvis points out in his recent book *Public Parts*, entrepreneurs must focus on the customer because he is one again king. Because of the internet, he often knows more about a product or idea than many of the people selling them.

Not to worry. Instead think untraditionally:
- Marketing: use blogs and social media to promote your products.
- Tools: most tools are Open Source and free. Microsoft offers free versions of applications like Word, Excel, and PowerPoint in the cloud.
- Infrastructure: More cloud goodness—you don't have to buy servers anymore.
- People: callous for me to say, but in a recession, people are free or cheap.
- Office space: what office space? You can work out of your garage, home office (like David Hewlett and Bill Packard), or just form a virtual team.
- Be careful of opening product locations. People are shifting to working and shopping from home. Physical locations are expensive.

The bottom line is this is one of the cheapest times to be an entrepreneur, so go into your garage and start prototyping.

Angel Capital

While I have stressed the use of angel capital; don't get me wrong. Raising funding is critical. Why? Because the #1 reason (by far) why entrepreneurs fail is that they don't have, or run out of, cash. But one thing I'd like to clarify is that you *can* start and grow a business without funding or with little funding. In fact, many great businesses have been started this way.

A survey of Inc. 500 companies found that 48% started with $20K in financing or less, and 73% started with less than $100K in financing. And, if you are looking for *big* funding sources, like venture capital, they will often want to see that you have bootstrapped or already raised other, smaller funding sources before they fund you. Rather, you must start by bootstrapping or raising enough funding to get you going, and then later on, many more funding sources will become available to you to help you grow your company.

Let me give you some examples of entrepreneurs who have done this. In fact, most of these entrepreneurs have started with these small amounts and then raised huge amounts of funding when they were ready for rapid growth:

- Armour's Kevin Plank funded his company's launch with credit cards.
- Brian Scudamore founded 1-800-GOT-JUNK, which now has over 200 franchised locations in the US alone, with just $700 of funding.
- Michael Dell launched Dell Computers with only $1,000.
- Jill Blashack Strahan launched Tastefully Simple, which offers easy-to-prepare foods and gifts with just $6,000 in savings. Her company now generates over $115 Million in annual revenues.
- Ben & Jerry launched with $8,000 in savings and a $4,000 loan.
- Pamela Skaist-Levy and Gela Nash-Taylor launched Juicy Couture Clothing with just $200 and a revolving line of credit. Juicy Couture was later sold for $53 million to Liz Claiborne.
- Google's Sergey Brin and Larry Page launched the company with credit cards (and later raised angel then VC funding among others).

And, in addition to these and other entrepreneurs who launched their companies with little funding, there are tons of entrepreneurs who have launched their companies with non-traditional sources of funding. Such as Kenneth Cole, who raised hundreds of thousands of dollars in funding from a shoe manufacturer (vendor funding). Or Blowfly Beer, who raised tens of thousands of dollars in funding from customers (customer financing).

The key point I want to stress here is that the vast majority of entrepreneurs have the mindset that if they can't raise money from banks, angels, or VCs, that they can't launch or grow their companies. This is simply *not* true. So don't fall into this thinking. Let's get XYZ profitable then go for funding for growth and expansion: a more compelling story. It may be that you need $50-100K to cushion yourself as you make XYZ profitable. You should, however, wrap your story around the areas we discussed: research, marketing etc.

Crowd Funding

I have talked before about "Angel investing" I do so again because I have identified the common characteristics of those entrepreneurs who successfully raise Angel funding known in the financial markets as Crowd funding:

1. They start by having their close friends and family members Crowd fund them. You see, if I as a stranger go to a Crowd funding project and see that no one else has funded it, I become skeptical. Conversely, if I see that 35 people have already funded it, I am more confident. This is called "social proof." Entrepreneurs who successfully raise Crowd funding leverage social proof by getting their close friends and family members to fund them before they promote their raise to strangers.

2. They offer "tangible" rewards. Most strangers won't fund you out of the goodness of their hearts; rather, they fund you to earn the rewards you have promised them. Such as you shipping them your $100 product later when they give you $65 in funding today. The more tangible your reward, and the more you can position it as something the customer wants, the more successful you will be.

3. They create a cool, personal video. Even if your product or service idea is great, most strangers won't want to fund you. But, if you create a video in which you are speaking about why you want to create the product/service, your success will skyrocket. In the video, you need to connect with people. You want to inspire strangers who watch it, so that they want to fund you and see you succeed, and they want to tell their friends about you.

4. They manage their Crowd funding raises from start to finish (which usually lasts 60 or 90 days). Once you set up your Crowd funding project, you're not quite done. You need to market it via social media and other channels (like PR which has worked really well for entrepreneurs raising Crowd funding). You need to respond to questions that potential funders pose. And if the amount of funding you initially sought gets ex-

ceeded (which fortunately happens a lot), you need to post new videos and updates telling strangers that you will accept more money and what you will use it for.

Ted Federici

CHAPTER TWO: PLANNING

Defining Success

I have seen it defined as consistently achieving your pre-determined goals. Others have said it's your level of "grit" or ability to fail consistently without losing your motivation or giving up from self-doubt. Your business goals and dreams are unique to you. While the object of success is different for every person, we have been able to determine the characteristics that are shared by those who have found success and fulfillment, as they define it.

The industries and pursuits of successful people are very diverse, so mimicking their actual day-to-day behavior is not always a true model of how to get what you want (unless you're trying to succeed at the same thing they are). Watching the actions of successful business people reveals their mindset that motivates them and, more importantly, gives them the perseverance and consistency to take the actions needed every day to achieve what they dream.

This is a humbling reminder that growing your business is more than just knowing what to do, or finding out the secret technique or method that will make you more money. While that helps in choosing your strategy and making the execution easier, the reality is that anyone with a strong enough success mindset will have the attributes needed to find out what to do, commit to it, and then get to work through thick and thin, changing their course as needed until they've realize their goal.

What are the elements of this "success mindset"? They are:

Confidence in your dream and your abilities. How strongly do you believe in your company's potential? How strongly do you believe that you have the knowledge and skills necessary to pull it off? This is self-confidence. Entrepreneurs who don't fully believe in themselves are more likely to quit, or make excuses that keep them from trying in the first place.

Part of confidence comes from experience. After all, if you've made money in business in the past, it's not too hard to see yourself doing it

27

again, or more of it. When you see your hunches pay off, you'll learn to trust your gut even more.

Another part of confidence is knowing that you are probably going to run into challenges and fail at a few things along the way. It means you can handle setbacks without questioning your own ability. There will always, I repeat, always be setbacks. The difference is that a confident entrepreneur knows he can figure out what to do when the time comes and overcome them.

My point here is that when things don't work out the way you planned, it does not mean that you are personally lacking in some way. The point is to achieve your goal, not to have a flawless plan.

Flexible and willing to learn. The sharpest entrepreneurs are continually learning from whatever source presents itself. This means getting expert knowledge in their field and learning how to run a business in general. But it also means listening along the way for ideas that you can implement directly in new or current projects. It doesn't matter who the ideas come from. Constantly look outside yourself for new ideas and be flexible. After all, there is no one right way to run your business, and copying your competitors exactly is more of an exercise in flattery than a strategy for success.

Your results are also a source of learning if you'll listen to them. This applies to both successes and failures. If you succeed at something, it's not because you're invincible—it's because you took certain actions that produced a certain result. Same goes for failures.

Focus more on actions and results and what they can teach you through trial and error, rather than making things personal.

Persistence and determination. The most persistent entrepreneur will usually win. There are plenty of talented, highly intelligent, and educated people out there. Why aren't they all successful? My guess would be their mindset. Perhaps they don't believe they can achieve what they want, or set their sights low to avoid the risk of failure and pain.

We can learn a lot from entrepreneurs like Henry Ford—a man(I have read) of average intelligence who surrounded himself with the very best people. His job was to consider their input and make decisions accordingly. People look to the leader to press forward; that's you!

So even if you don't currently have the know-how or the funds (or whatever you think is holding you back) to achieve your dream right now, know that you will eventually if you continue to make proactive efforts towards your goal. It's just a matter of time!

Focused concentration. Ask any fighter and he'll tell you that focus and concentration are crucial to success. Would you want to get distracted by shiny objects in the crowd if you were in the middle of a heavyweight battle? You'd probably get your clock cleaned, or at least fail to be effective at attacking. Why would your business be any less important? Every day, you will have a ton of information, thoughts, and cries for your attention coming at you. The average person comes in contact with as many as 2,000 advertising messages per day, for example.

How well do you focus on your goals? Do you review them often? Do you make plans for their achievement, and revise them when they don't work as well as you thought? At any given hour of your workday, ask yourself, "What am I doing right now, and is it helping me achieve my goal or is it busy work, a distraction, or something I could delegate?" The topics of confidence and self-esteem as well as mindfulness and concentration are not only fascinating studies in self-knowledge. They can help you make money. They can help you grow your business, and find success. To apply this, take a look at your own mindset lately. Has it been conducive to success, or do you find yourself getting in your own way? The process of developing the right mindset is not as simple as a one-time task list. It's based on setting the habit of consistently paying attention to your thoughts and feelings, which reveal your higher thought patterns and beliefs.

Obstacles to Strategic Thinking

Obviously, every business needs a *vision*—a clear definition of what you'd like your business to become in the future. And, every business needs a set *strategy*—a definition and plan of how your business is going to reach this vision.

All the key elements—what you sell, to whom, for how much, what you promise, etc.—they are part of your company's strategy or direction towards creating the business you want.

When you've chosen a direction and vision, the next step is strategic planning—mapping out how you will achieve this over a long-term time frame (usually one year). This, like all planning, involves determining what projects (I call them Strategies) you will complete and when, and how you will allocate resources such as man-hours, money, and assets.

Lastly, your strategic plan will break down into specific, detailed short-term tactics that help you know what to do on a month-to-month and even day-to-day basis.

But can you imagine what happens when you have a short-term plan to handle all the business and projects you have going on, but no longer-term, strategic plan to tie it all together? Maybe you've experienced it...the answer is chaos, drudgery, and endless wheel-spinning with no little progress.

So, let me explain some of the key errors and obstacles facing entrepreneurs and what to do about them:

Unclear, Unshared Vision
With all the time team members spend together in meetings and talking to each other, it's surprising how often they come away with different mental pictures of what the company is supposed to be and in what direction it's supposed to be going.
Everyone sees the company's future from their own perspective and function. It's your job to repeatedly communicate your company's vision and strategy to them—50 or 100 times if you have to—so they're all on the same page and can give you better advice and support.

Operational Thinking Dominates Your Time

This happens when most of the time spent in meetings is discussing *how* to run the business and putting out the fires that come up so often. Rather than also spending time strategizing and planning.

It's easier said than done to carve out time in your schedule for strategic thinking and planning, but that's the nature of entrepreneurship—taking care of today's business with an eye on the future. *Hard to do, but keep in mind that delegating more of the day-to-day operational tasks to your team can free you up to do the strategic work, which may be something that only you can do.*

I have to admit, when you show up for work it's easy to turn your attention first to all of the urgent tasks and demands for your time. Strategic thinking, on the other hand, is one of those activities that time management gurus classify as "Important, but not Urgent" (an example of "urgent" being something you *must* deal with immediately like an irate customer on the phone).

This means you have to *fight* for your strategic time, as it's the process that takes an unfocused business and sets it firmly on the track to success. Block it out on your calendar—each week, schedule time to assess and/or discuss strategy.

Getting Complacent When Things Are Good

Paul Lemberg, a management guru whom I admire, refers to the Comfort Zone phenomenon as leading business managers to become "fat, dumb, and happy." In other words, becoming complacent when things are going fine. This can lead to becoming reactive with your strategy, rather than proactive. Do you want to be reconfiguring your company and innovating under duress at breakneck speed at the last minute, or well ahead of time when the pressure is off?

Quite a few companies wait until a crisis comes around to kick-start their strategic thinking out of necessity. You don't want to be planning during a crisis.

Wasting Time With 5-Year Plans

Let's be honest here. Isn't a five-year pretty much a one-year plan, plus four years of guessing?

You *must* have a clear vision of what your company will be like in five years, but to try and guess the details of what will be going on in 43 months, for example, in a fast-changing world is wishful thinking.

But once again, you must create your long-term (5-year) vision, which will guide all of your annual and other planning. Take a sheet of paper and describe the key elements of what you'd like your business to do, be, and look like in five years. Document this and use it to judge new opportunities and directions to see how well they fit.

Planning Once Per Year, Out of Routine

We all know how around New Year's day, many individuals start thinking about their personal goals for the year ahead. And many businesses work hard on a yearly plan during the same month of every year. But can you wait to do your strategic thinking until your annual cycle calls for it? The business environment just isn't that predictable.

I suggest writing up your strategic plan right now and then making periodic changes throughout the year. You must set your annual plan, and then judge your progress and adjust your strategy and plan as needed.

No Process or Methodology for Strategic Planning

I suggest that you discuss and choose your *strategy* in one session, then do your full *strategic planning* in another. In setting *strategy*, you'll be in creative mode, exploring all possible options. Choose the strategy that makes the most sense, and then figure out the precise *action plan* to achieve it in a separate, more analytical meeting.

With appropriate time set aside for strategic thinking and planning, and by avoiding the obstacles discussed herein, you'll experience the joy that comes from knowing exactly what you're striving for and how to get there. You'll feel more grounded, balanced, and centered. You'll come to work with greater purpose and passion. And you'll have more to show for your efforts at the end of each year.

I am a firm believer in strategic planning and creating the time to accomplish. One or two days in a year for you and your team to step back and lay out your future and the year you are in is not too much to ask. I stand ready to guide you.

Ted Federici

Strategies for Success

For over 20 years, I've been a serial entrepreneur. Not all of my ventures have been successful, but the majority of them have been. Someone recently asked me to list the keys to my success. Upon thinking about it, I identified the seven strategies I religiously use, and which I attribute to my success. Read them and use them yourself, and I'm confident the level of your success will increase dramatically.

1. Have a Clear Vision of Where You Want to Go
If you don't have a clear picture of the company you want to build, there's no way you can build it. Spend time figuring out the precise attributes of the business you would like to build. How much will your revenues be? What products and services will you be offering customers? How many employees will you have? And, by what date will you achieve all this?

2. Have a Written Strategic Plan
Your vision is your dream. And to attain the dream, you need a *strategic plan* that details how you will achieve it. Among other things, it must document your product strategy, your marketing strategy and your human resource strategy. Your plan should detail your long-term vision, but focus more specifically on what you must accomplish in the next year.

3. Have Quarterly, Monthly, Weekly, And Daily Goals
If you were able to draw a line from where you are now to where you want your company to be, that line would be known as a trajectory. Success is about getting on the right trajectory. That is, as long as what you accomplish today, this week, this month, and this year progresses you farther and farther along the line (versus going below the line or stagnating), then you will eventually reach your long-term goal.

To stay on the right trajectory, you must set quarterly, monthly, weekly, and daily goals. Each goal should be set with an understanding of the larger goal. For example, figure out what you need to accomplish this quarter in order to properly progress towards your annual goal. And then figure out what you need to accomplish this month to properly progress towards your quarterly goal. And so on. By creating and achieving these smaller, periodic goals, you start to ride the trajectory to your ultimate vision.

4. Educate Yourself Continually

To succeed you need to continually invest in educating yourself. You should be reading the right books. You should be attending the right seminars, conferences, and trade shows. And you must read the right newspapers, magazines, newsletters, and blogs.

Do not skimp on spending money on educating yourself. Investing in your education (and that of your key employees) will generally give you a larger return on investment than anything else in your business.

5. Satisfy Your Customers

Satisfied customers are the key to your success. If you can't satisfy customers, you will fail. They say it takes one dissatisfied customer to undo the good that nine happy ones provide by spreading the word about their experience with you friend-to-friend or in online reviews.

You can satisfy your customers on the front end (at or immediately after the time of the first sale) by making the sales and delivery process smooth and seamless, by reducing the customer's participation or steps required to use the product, by managing their expectations so that what they get is exactly what they were promised, and of course with spectacular customer service and support. In addition to providing a great experience as just specified, the product or service you deliver them should be high quality and fully satisfy them.

6. Market to Your Customers

This is a big one, particularly since most business owners don't do it enough. Most entrepreneurs and business owners are so focused on getting new customers that they neglect their current customers. And, unlike prospective customers, current customers have a track record of buying from you, and are much more likely to buy from you again than prospective customers.

So spend time listening to and communicating with your current customers. Find out what that truly want and need, and stay top-of-mind so they buy from you again and again.

7. Be Laser-Focused in Your Work

This ties in with number 3 (Have Quarterly, Monthly, Weekly, and Daily Goals), but deserves its own mention. Which is this: be sure to focus on one aspect of your business at a time. Conversely, trying to do too many things at one will diffuse your focus and inevitably result in failure.

Limit the number of projects you're working on until they are finished. Remember, twenty projects that are 99% complete but not live yield less revenue that just one project that is 100% complete and live. As we keep hearing from politicians, you, the entrepreneurs and small business owners, are the backbone of our economy. Follow these strategies and you'll be more successful, and so will the economy!

Success in Reverse

When starting a business, most entrepreneurs dream about the finish line—specifically how their lives will be radically better once their business becomes a huge success. But, soon after they start their businesses, entrepreneurs/business owners become trapped in the day-to-day, week-to-week, and month-to-month goals of generating more sales and profits, improving employee performance, and trying to reduce their hours and stress. At some point, the vast majority of entrepreneurs become 100% focused on these short-term goals and lose sight of their long-term visions. As a result, they begin to wander, and never achieve the vision they initially hoped to achieve.

The solution is rather simple: you need to stop what you're doing and dream again about the finish line. Specifically, you need to reassess what it is that you're trying to accomplish with your business. In many cases, this long-term vision will be the same as the long-term vision you had when you started your business. In other cases, your long-term vision might have changed. But in *every* case, you must reassess what your long-term vision is, or you'll have virtually no chance of achieving it. And importantly, once you identify this vision, you need to reverse engineer it.

That's right, you need to fully imagine how your business will look once you have achieved your long-term vision, and then create the action plan for achieving it. For example, if your dream includes a company with 300 employees, you need to create the plan now for hiring and training these employees. To help you achieve this, follow my step by step plan below for identifying your long-term vision and reverse engineering it.

1. Identify Your Long-Term Vision
Write down what your ultimate goal is for your business.
For example, do you want to sell it to another company? Sell/give it to your employees or children? Take it public? Continue to run it forever and reap ongoing profits?

2. Identify Your Key End-game Metrics
By what date would you like your vision to be achieved?

What will your company's annual revenues be at this date?

How many customers will you have at this date?

How many employees will you have at this date?

On this date, what will your day to day responsibilities be?

On this date, what will be your top selling products and/or services?

3. Reverse Engineer Success Within the Key Functional Areas

Answer the following questions as if today were the future date in which you achieved your long-term vision and you were looking backwards.

Marketing:

What marketing channels allowed you to attract/gain the most customers?

What have you done to fully satisfy your customers?

What business partnerships (if any) have you forged that have resulted in significant numbers of new clients?

R&D:

What have you done to develop your top selling products and/or services?

Human Resources:

Who are your key managers that motivate and manage your other employees?

When did you find these key managers?

Where did you find them?

How did you develop them?

When did you start ramping up your hiring process?

Operations:

What systems have you built to ensure your business runs smoothly and without your required day-to-day involvement?

Finance:

Who funded you along the way?

How did you meet these funding sources?

4: Create Your Action Plans

Create action plans from your answers above. For example, if you answered "direct mail" as your top marketing channel, document your direct mail strategy. Document who you will mail to, what your message will be, what your direct mail timeline will be, etc.

The exercise above is critical in ensuring your success. The key is to not only dream about what your business looks like when it has achieved success, but to reverse engineer that dream. You need to think through how your business got to its successful state. And then work backwards in creating action plans that will get you there. Once you create these action plans, be sure that you and your team stay focused on executing them.

Ted Federici

Most Businesses Fail

Most businesses fail. I hate to be so blunt, but this is the truth. The only thing that varies is just how many businesses fail. According to research I read recently from the University of Tennessee, 44% of businesses fail within the first three years. And within certain sectors, like information (which includes most technology companies), 63% fail within 3 years, or in Retail, 53% fail within 36 months. On the other hand, according to research from Bradley University, 70% to 80% of new businesses fail within their first year. Bradley University also found that half of those who survive the first year would fail within the next four years.

What is the number one cause of this failure? According to Dun & Bradstreet, the primary cause is lack of business planning. Yes, entrepreneurs and business owners don't plan to fail. Rather, they fail to plan (which causes them to fail).

In my view, there are two types of business plans: 1. The one you develop when you start your business; and 2. The one you develop to grow your business.

When you start your company, the purpose of your business plan is to ensure you have fully thought through your venture. Among other things, this plan includes significant market research. It assesses your market size to ensure the opportunity is big enough. It analyzes customer segments to confirm that customer needs match your company's proposed product and/or service offerings. And it analyzes the competition to determine how your company will position itself and how you will most effectively compete.

From a strategic standpoint, the business plan must document your marketing plan (how you will secure customers), your human resources plan (who you will hire) and your operations plan (what key milestones you will accomplish and when). When you're done, your business plan will confirm your market opportunity and give you a roadmap to follow. It will also be required should you wish to gain funding from investors and lenders.

Once your business is up and running, you still need a business plan in order to succeed. This is the second type of business plan, and I refer to this type of plan as a "strategic plan." I term it as such because this type of plan requires much less research (since you already know who your customers are, the market fundamentals, and lots of information about your competitors). Rather, the focus of this plan is strategy.

Specifically, this plan needs to identify precisely:

- Where you want your company to be in five years,
- What you need to accomplish within the next year to progress you to that point, and
- What are the few critical success factors.
- What is your strategy is to complete your key milestones to meet the critical success factors in the next 12 months.

In determining the optimal strategies, you need to consider your company's strengths, and opportunities that can best leverage them. If you don't take time to do this, you become too tactical. That is, you continue to use the same tactics that have gotten you to the point you are at. And often times, the strategy and tactics that got you where you are today are *not* the strategy and tactics that will get you to the next level. Spend time figuring out the best strategies to follow. The good news is that you've already proven you can execute on strategies (which is what got you to where you are now).

After you figure out the big picture opportunities to go after (which often fall into the categories of further penetrating your existing market, going after a new market, or creating new products/services for existing and/or new markets), you need to revisit the core strategies you developed in your initial business plan.

To start, you need to modify your marketing plan. Importantly, your marketing plan should always be adding new marketing venues or channels (e.g., direct mail, print, radio, search engine optimization, etc.) as the more channels you have, the more customers you will get and the less risk you have of one channel losing effectiveness. For example, think about businesses who used to get all or the majority of their customers from the yellow pages; many of these companies have perished.

Next, consider your human resources strategy. What new people will you need to hire to accomplish your key goals in the coming years? In what areas will you need people, and what skill sets must they have?

And finally, you need to develop your operations strategy. Figure out what key tasks and milestones you need to accomplish over the next year and break them down into smaller projects that you and your team must accomplish. And then create a master schedule showing who owns what, and how and when these projects will be completed (I like using a Gantt chart to do this).

Creating a business plan when you start your company and annually creating strategic plans to grow your company is absolutely essential to your success. Research proves it. If you want to avoid failure, and achieve maximum success, make sure you are continuously creating, updating and following your business and strategic plans.

A Thriving Business Could Bankrupt You

I encourage you to think about your business a little differently. That is, I want you to think about it as a product. And specifically, a product that one day you might sell to an acquirer (for a lot of money, of course).

By thinking about your business this way, you will be more likely to build a company that an acquirer would want to buy. As opposed to the vast number of un-sellable businesses most entrepreneurs unfortunately create. Importantly, even if your intention is never to sell your business, I want you to adapt this way of thinking. Because the same attributes that will make your business attractive to buyers will also make it perform better for you. Remember, your business should work for you, not the opposite.

Looking at your business as a product, the first question to ask (and the first question an acquirer will ask) is:

Does the company you built stand out from the others? In assessing a product, we typically consider its unique attributes or unique selling proposition. For your business, what about it will get the buyers' attention? Will it be your cash flow, recurring revenues, or potential for significant future growth? A second question a product buyer might ask is "'how easy is it to use the product?"

Similarly, an acquirer will ask: How easy will it be to run this business after acquisition? Clearly, the acquirer will want the smoothest transition possible when taking over. The acquirer does *not* want to deal with the following:

- Employees not knowing what to do or how to do it without you being there
- Clients and customers leaving along with you/the old owner
- Hit-or-miss revenues and unpredictable cash flow
- Being outdated by competition, trends, government regulations and/or new technologies

Likewise an acquirer would *not* want to purchase a company in which a small handful of clients represented the majority of revenues. In such a case, even just one or two clients leaving could materially hurt revenues and possibly bankrupt the company. Yes, even thriving businesses have been bankrupted by one or two trophy customers leaving because they failed to diversify their customer base.

Another question a product buyer typically asks is "what are the key features of the product that allow it to perform?" In relation to your business, these features include the Financial Metrics you've achieved and Business Assets you've built.

How has your business performed financially? Obviously a buyer will want a business that makes money (or could make it money), and the more predictable and turnkey it is, the more you can make from the sale. Doing your homework on what similar businesses sell for will help you plan your exit in this regard. Find out what yearly revenues and earnings is the "sweet spot" for businesses or individuals on your target acquirer list, and make this your revenue goal to shoot for before selling.

This is harder to do in the "survival" stage of your business, obviously. But over time as you discover what works and what doesn't and double up on what's effective, a higher percentage of your efforts will succeed and that adds to its predictability and stability.

What business assets has your company built? A big part of your business' value is the time and effort you put into building the business assets that allow your company to profitably and efficiently run. These business assets, which will strengthen your business and increase its value, include:

- Subscribers & Customers. Your customer base is one of your biggest assets and represents the chance to market repeatedly to the same people. Your databases of those who subscribe to be contacted by you via email, Facebook, text messages, etc, are also assets to spend time and energy increasing.
- Systems. Who does what in your business? What are the recurring tasks that someone will need to perform over and over and over again? What is the correct process for each of these, and the steps involved? Your business' acquirer does not want to come on board with all of this information in your head alone. Ideally, these processes and checklists will have been mapped out in advance and followed as "the way we do things here" all along.
- Solid team. It takes time, trial, and error to find the right team.

And it requires much more time after that to coach and develop them to be able to run the business without you. This is also part of the work involved with preparing a company for sale. Between documenting systems and this, having exceptional people is much more important, because the right people will be willing and able figure out how to get results without having it all spelled out.

- Hard assets and technology. These business assets include real estate, machinery, inventory, web properties, software, etc. which help you run the business more effectively.

A final question you might consider when purchasing a product, and particularly an investment product, is its future growth potential. When considering purchasing a company, a similar question the acquirer will ask is: What are the odds of sustainable future growth?

Few buyers are going to pay you a significant multiple of your annual revenues or profits unless they believe they can increase those revenues/profits even more. Otherwise, how are they going to get a return on their investment?

The ideal time to sell is after you have demonstrated profits and growth, and right as you're positioned to grow even more, and that means:

- Growth. Having a solid business model and proven lead generation strategies in place that can be expanded by increasing ad spend, or reaching new segments, or moving into entirely new markets altogether. Get your company in a position to do these things to pave the way for the new owner. Buyers also want a sales process and team that can handle several times more sales without a lot more training and development.
- Risk. What risks exist now or in the near future that might keep the new buyer from getting what they want? You'll want to consider ways to mitigate legal, financial, competitive, governmental, and technological changes and threats.
- Unique Competitive Advantage. Being a "me-too" company puts you on shaky footing, whether managing or selling such a business. Creating and cementing your unique competitive advantage is a critical factor in creating a quality business.

By looking at your business as a product, you can build a thriving enterprise that satisfies your needs and the needs of a big-pocketed acquirer. Specifically, you want to build your business so that it's unique, can run easily upon acquisition, has strong financial performance, includes valuable business assets, and is positioned for future growth. Do this and then enjoy the success that comes with it!

Outsourcing Mistakes

In today's business environment, you absolutely must outsource to stay competitive. No, I'm not talking about outsourcing your core competencies. But I am talking about outsourcing those business functions and activities that someone else can do faster, cheaper and/or more easily than you.

Unfortunately, when they start outsourcing, most entrepreneurs and small business owners make several mistakes. In this essay, I'm going to outline the most common mistakes made when outsourcing work or projects to freelancers or other service providers not on your internal team —I use the term "freelancers" below to describe folks to whom you outsource.

Use this as a quick checklist to run through when setting up your next outsourcing project. For each of these, think of how you will address or avoid these mistakes in advance to ensure smooth sailing.

Mistake #1: Having an undefined task/project. This is something I would do before even posting the project (i.e., to find the outsourced candidate) because you need to really understand the project in order to write an accurate job description. The process of defining the task/project clearly will also help you to estimate the costs, time frame, and skills needed from the person you hire. One way to do this is to write down a very clear and descriptive explanation of the task. Another way is to record yourself speaking the description. Finally, another great way is to take a screen recording of yourself doing the work you wish to outsource (or take a video of you doing the work if it's not computer based).

Mistake #2: Not having a well-planned estimate of costs. The more clearly you can define exactly what you need done by breaking it into parts, the better you can estimate how much time it will take - and therefore how much it will cost at the person's typical hourly rate. You don't want to just hand a bunch of work to someone and then get surprised when you get their bill and/or incorrectly assume they took too long to complete a project. If the project you need completed is something that requires specialized knowledge, describe the project to potential freelancers and get their opinion on what is really involved and how long it should take. If there's no typical hourly rate for the work they're doing, then just get a solid estimate of the total project cost and consider it to see if it makes sense compared to the revenue it should generate (or costs it should save).

Mistake #3: Not knowing your timeframe for starting and finishing the work. If you've ever provided services for a client in a rush, you know how stressful it can be to drop everything at the last minute and make their emergency yours. The people you outsource to are no different, and it will benefit you to plan and begin things in advance and not wait until the last minute. So for whatever work it is you want to do, figure out how long it will take and when it absolutely has to be completed. You'll come out with a rough idea of when the work needs to commence. Then, give yourself a week or two before that to post projects, screen candidates, and choose the right person or people.

Mistake #4: Hiring someone without enough experience. Nothing is worse than the blind leading the blind. When I hire someone to do something that I do not know how to do personally, they need to know how to do it, period. They need to educate you on their chosen skill set, not the other way around. Your role is to describe the end result you want, ask for and listen to their suggestions, and rely on their expertise and talent to achieve it according to your description.

Mistake #5: Not screening or testing enough freelancers. In choosing the right candidate, I would rather have more options to choose from than fewer. I would rather have 30 applicants and choose from among the top three than to have 10 applicants and choose from among the top one. Also, your goal is to build a list of qualified people to contact whenever you need them for projects or ongoing work. So even if you post a project and only hire one person, keep tabs of the runner-ups so to contact or test later on for future projects.

Mistake #6: Choosing someone with no room to grow. If you are outsourcing a project that you know you'll need again in the future (e.g., graphic design), you want to have one eye on the present project and the other on your future needs. Think about what similar services you'll need in the future and to what extent? Or, if you have a freelancer build something that, once done, needs maintenance, then be sure to ask them about their work hours and schedule. Find out if they have enough time left for your needs in addition to their other clients. It's terrible to go back to a great freelancer later on who is apologetic but too busy to help you.

Mistake #7: Holding on to your weaknesses. If your business is weak in a certain area, it may also be weak at managing someone performing the work outside of your company, too. Think about it: every worthwhile endeavor requires some basic knowledge and strategy, as well as some understanding of how to perform the work and measure the results. At least get this working knowledge upfront so that you can be effective at managing your freelancers. It doesn't matter if someone else is doing the work or not; if you don't start the project with a clear outcome and strategy, and continue to stay on top of it (not washing your hands and hiding somewhere) it will fail regardless of the skills and intelligence of your outsourcers.

Mistake #8: Lack of communication. You heard of management by walking around. Well, this is called seagull management. A seagull manager will be gone for days on end and suddenly come sailing in with the wind, squawking and dropping tons of work on everybody, and then flying away not to be seen again for days or weeks on end. What seagull managers don't realize is that you have to constantly be there for your team. This doesn't mean it needs to take a lot of time, but they would appreciate fast responses just as you like them from others. Again, just because someone else is performing the work does not mean you can abdicate your responsibility to support and manage them to achieve the result.

Mistake #9: Insufficient feedback. If you plan on using your freelancer for more than just a few quick tasks, then you will want to invest in your relationship with them from the beginning. Your job as a manager is to coach them and help them to do things exactly as you want over time. You should expect them to make mistakes and encourage them to fail quickly so you can give feedback and show how to do it the right way.

Don't be a perfectionist, and don't make them afraid or hesitant to admit challenges or mistakes and then blame them later. Many managers just assume that the people who are working for them can read their minds and know all the little details without being told. This is not true, even when the person is highly intelligent. It's your job to communicate clearly and often.

Mistake #10: Underutilizing hired talent. This probably keeps most entrepreneurs and small business owners from outsourcing in the first place. As entrepreneurs, I have to admit that we can have some pretty big egos. While this helps in the vision and confidence departments, it can also lead to the "no one can do it as well as I can" syndrome. Maybe not, but I would still rather have 10 people who are 80% as good as me doing 90% of the work. Think about it! Besides, with proper coaching and support, you can make a good person great-as long as they are coachable and motivated to grow. And even when you are outsourcing work to someone, don't miss opportunities to give them even more work once they have proven themselves with some smaller task. I like to list all the work required on a consistent basis and check the sub-items off as I outsource them, one at a time.

Implement these suggestions and your outsourcing experience will be a lot more effective and hassle-free!

CHAPTER 3:
EXECUTING FOR GROWTH

Do You Have a Growth Strategy?

If you were to ask ten people in your organization to define the word, "strategy," chances are you'd probably get between eight and ten different answers ranging from, "a plan," to, "a series of tactics," to, "something management does to justify their salaries." It is an interesting observation to make because if strategy is so fundamental to the success of any business or organization, one would think that there ought to be more clarity around the concept. But there isn't.

However, before I define what I believe strategy is, let me clarify what it isn't (and why I'm pretty confident that your "strategy" probably isn't one). The biggest misconception I've encountered about strategy is that it's synonymous with long-range planning (it isn't). In fact, for most organizations, their "strategic plan" isn't very strategic, it's simply a long-range plan.

In other words, throwing the word "strategic" in front of the word "plan," does not make a plan any more strategic than throwing the word "friendly" in front of the word "service" makes your local cable company representative friendly. To help you see how important this distinction is between strategy and planning, I'd like to share with you four key distinctions between strategy and tactics (tactics being the sub-points of a plan).

1. Strategy is about direction; tactics are about action. Strategy seeks to answer the question, "What do we want to be?" Whereas tactics answer the question of, "How are we going to get there?" In other words, strategy isn't about how to, it's about want to.

Strategy points out a direction for an organization. It tells everyone, "This is where we're headed and here are the boundaries in which we're going to play on our way there." True strategy work doesn't tell anyone, "Here's what we need to do next week." Nor does it say, "Next year we'll sell x number of widgets." However, it might tell us, "To fulfill our mission and vision, we need to add x (another revenue stream) to our product

50

mix," or "We need to change our market segment," or "We're a product-driven company, not a method of distribution company (or vice versa)."

2. Strategy focuses on the future, tactics focus on the present. Strategy always looks at the future, and then looks back to the present, whereas tactics always look at where we are (the present) and then project into the future—which is a huge difference. For example, a strategic decision might be to completely cut off a line of business, not because it's failing, but because it's not where the company is headed. Whereas a tactical plan will always start with the current lines of business and figure out how to make each one of them incrementally better. In other words, tactical plans usually only lead to incremental improvement, whereas real strategic formulations can/should radically change and accelerate the growth of the organization because they're not hindered by current "realities."

3. Strategy is an executive function; tactics are an operational function. Strategy formulation is the big picture work that top-level executives must be involved in. This is the work that determines the nature and direction of an organization. However, planning and tactics are operational responsibilities and therefore should be developed by those who are responsible for implementing them. Or to put it another way, strategy is best done "top down," whereas tactics are best done from the "bottom up." So, once the executive team has developed an organization's strategy, those who are most closely responsible for the results ought to be involved in setting the tactics necessary for achieving the strategy that the executive team set.

4. Strategy is about perception; tactics are about execution. Strategy defines how an organization wants to be perceived in the marketplace (as the organization that best provides the products and/or services that its market needs/wants/desires). Tactics figure out how to be best execute that strategy (i.e. how are we going to get there). Or to put it another way, strategy work is about developing and gaining clarity about an organization's competitive advantages so that it can communicate those differences. Whereas tactics are focused on the steps to ensure that those differences do exist.

That said, I know there are some (okay, many) who would eagerly jump past strategy formulation work in order to jump right into tactical work. Why? Because they want action. They want to know what they can start doing tomorrow in order to make what they're doing better. However, the obvious problem with that mindset is, "It doesn't matter how fast you're going, if you're going in the wrong direction." In other words, if the strategy isn't right, the tactics probably won't be right either.

So, as you review the four differences between strategy and tactics, is your "strategic plan" really strategic? Or is it simply a long-range plan dressed up in a fancier title? If you want to accelerate your organization's growth, then you'll want to take the time to do real strategy work. Why? Because when everyone is clear on where you're headed, the "how to get there's" become obvious and you'll end up getting where you want to go faster, with less friction and more joy.

Oh, and one last thing, if you're wondering how I would define strategy, here's my definition, "Strategy is a framework that guides the choices an organization makes about its nature and direction, as well as its operational activities and tactics." Strategy isn't a plan, it's an intentionally designed-framework that helps everyone in an organization know how to make choices about both what to do and what not to do on their way toward fulfilling the mission and vision of that organization. Done right, it makes everything easier!

Ted Federici

Want to Grow Your Business?

If you want to grow your business significantly faster, you have to learn to think differently. In other words, if you grew at 7.7% last year, chances are you'll grow at the same rate or lower, unless something significantly changes. This is one of the reasons why I love Nicholas Negroponte's line, "Incrementalism is innovation's greatest enemy."

Small incremental changes rarely lead to any significant break-throughs. Doing more of the same, "just a little bit better," rarely sets the world on fire. So, how do you get out of this rut?

Well, one way is to come up with a mental construct that forces you to think differently—at a much higher level. And one of those constructs is to practice what I like to call, "The Double It Game."

There are a number of different ways to play this game.

1. Let's say you want to grow by 20% this year. Instead of thinking about how to grow by 20%, "Double It" and figure out how to grow by 40%.

2. Or let's say you're a $3M company. Instead of planning for 20% growth this year, why not double your annual revenue and ask the question, "What if we were a $6M company?"

3. Or, let's say you are closing 50 deals a month. Instead of thinking, "How can I close 60 deals a month?" why not "Double It" and ask, "How can I close100 sales per month?"

You can play the "Double It" game with a whole variety of different areas in your business. However, the point of this exercise isn't to suggest that your budget, sales, or annual revenues should be double.

In fact, it's usually wiser to be a little conservative on budget numbers and projections. The point of the exercise is to force you to think differently—and in the process discover some ideas that might radically accelerate the growth of your business.

When you play The Double It Game, chances are you'll discover things like the following:

- As a leader, your job will have to change, and you'll probably need to delegate out a lot more

- You'll probably need to invest more in staff training
- You'll probably force yourself to realize there are some staff you need to let go of now
- You probably have some staff whom you'll need to transition out over the next year
- You'll need to recruit some better talent
- Your business model may need to change
- Your sales process will need to change
- You'll need to add some new product and service lines (while killing others)
- You'll need to open up some new markets (and bring in new people who can do that)
- You'll probably need to either store some cash or acquire some new capital in order to expand faster

At twice your size or at twice your growth rate, almost everything has to change. Management guru Peter Drucker used to say that every time an organization grows by 45%, it has to change its organizational structure. At a Double It rate, that means every year, everything will probably have to change. So, what would that look like? That is the heart of the "Double It" question.

What would your business (or organization) look like if it were twice as large at the end of this year (as it is in the beginning)? What would be different about you and your role? Your staff? Your management? Your operations? Your marketing and sales? Your cash flow? Sounds like a fun question to ponder, doesn't it? It is! So, go to it. Your future waits!

Frankly, you cannot afford not to think about it! If you are not growing, you will eventually go out of business. Importantly, on a related note, in order to grow your business, you need to consider what you must *stop* doing.

You see, the natural tendency for most owners and CEOs of SMBs (small and medium-sized businesses), who want to grow their businesses (or organizations) is to keep adding more and more to their plates. Every new book or conference or webinar suggests a new tactic that can "help grow your business," so they keep adding. Unfortunately that strategy simply makes most of us feel overwhelmed. It makes us too busy, unfocused and keeps us from doing the things we ought to be doing to actually grow our businesses.

For example, I was coaching a CEO who got embroiled in an internal issue that was sucking time away from him. In the early days of his business, this was the kind of issue he would have needed to handle. But at this stage, he shouldn't have been involved in this issue at all. So, I simply said, as he was recounting his past few days, "Who should have been dealing with this?" He got the point. It wasn't that he was doing something bad. It was that he was still thinking like the CEO of a smaller company—and still doing some of the things he used to do-even though his company had grown beyond him needing to do them.

Sound Familiar? The reality is that every leader faces the same dilemma. If you're doing your job well, your business or organization should be growing. If it's growing, more and more will land on your plate—unless you're extremely diligent and intentional about getting as much as possible off your plate.

One of my favorite sayings is, "You have to subtract before you add." To simply keep adding more and more to your plate (or to your organization's) without subtracting somewhere first is a recipe for disaster.

Here's what I'd recommend. Take a look at your last few weeks' to do's (or calendars):

1. What did you do that someone else could have done at 80% (or more) of your capabilities?

2. What meetings did you attend that you really shouldn't attend any more?

3. What people did you take calls from or meet with that you shouldn't any more?

4. Which emails did you respond to that someone else should have handled?

5. What items do you know you should delegate to someone else that you keep doing (just because you like doing them)?

Be ruthless. Nothing changes until something changes! If you want to lead a larger business (or organization), you have to give up more and more of the things you used to do and focus more and more on just a few key items that can deliver significant growth gains. So, what do you need to stop doing?

Who Do You Need to Become to Grow Your Business?

When we are about to kick off a new year, I often ask a client, "how are you feeling"? If you're like most of the business people I interact with, you're probably feeling pretty excited but anxious. Hey, when you have 360 plus days in front of you, anything is possible. I find myself continually asking one key question, "Who do you need to become to generate the kinds of results you want?" Now, why is that question so critical? Because history teaches us that most of us will end one year, similar to the year before. Why? Because we reproduce not what we want, we reproduce *who we are*. I don't care about your level of results. You could be generating $250K, $2.5M or $25M. Whatever that number is, it's a reflection of who you are as the leader of your business.

Let's just pick a $1M business to make this simple. There are a lot of people who have businesses well under $1M a year. The fact that you're at $1M says a lot about you. Chances are you think, act, and feel a lot differently than the people who are making $100K per year—and you know that.

Furthermore, let's suppose that you've been hovering around $1M for the past three years. So, what makes you think this year will be any different? Your plan may call for a 15%, 20% or 30% increase (or more), but what makes you think that will happen? The past three years you've set similar goals and nothing has changed. Why? Because, for good or for bad, everything always flows down from the person at the top of any business or organization.

Who you are as a strategist, leader, manager, marketer, and money manager sets the high water mark for your business. In other words, the key to growing your business faster is to make sure that you're growing *you* ahead of your business.

The harsh reality for all of us who lead businesses and organizations is that, at the end of the day, we're responsible for the growth or plateau or decline of our businesses or organizations. That is because they're always a direct reflect of us.

Back to my original question. If you want to grow your business or organization, how are you going to change *you*? Who do you need to become to be the person to lead a $1.3M vs. a $1M business or, even better, to lead a $2M business. You need to change ahead of your business.

To make this incredibly practical, here's what I'd recommend. Take out a sheet of paper (or open a mind map on your computer) and put a circle in the middle. In the middle of the circle write, "Who Do I Need to Become to Lead a _____ Business? (Insert your revenue number for the blank.)

Next, if you want to create change with anything in life, there are only four options (more, less, start, stop). Write these four options out like four spokes on a wheel and then write your answers out from each of the four main spokes. What are the four options that form the four main spokes?

1. What do I need to *stop* doing that I'm already doing? No matter what your level of success is, there are things you're doing that *you* shouldn't be doing. You could stop them completely. You could delegate them away. You could outsource them. But, to get to the next level, there are some things you have to stop doing. If you've been following me for any time, you know I keep saying, "Before you can add anything to your plate, you need to subtract first." So, what do you need to stop doing this year that you were doing last year?

2. What do I need to *start* doing that I'm not currently doing? This list is usually a little easier than the last one (though the last one is more important). To get a new result, you know you need to do new things. What are you going to start doing this year in order to function at a higher level?

3. What do I need to do *less* of that I'm currently doing? Though this sounds similar to question number one, it's not, In other words, there are some things that you're currently doing that you shouldn't stop (like responding to email) but that you should do less of (like not checking it 20 times a day). Therefore, what do you need to do less of this year if you want to become the kind of person who can deliver the kinds of results you want?

4. What do I need to do *more* of that I'm currently doing? Once you get past the administrivia, chances are there are some very good things you're

already doing that if you did them more often, would help you become a better leader of your business.

For example, delegation. Most owners and entrepreneurs know the concept or idea of delegation, and occasionally do it, but if they want to get to the next level, they need to do more of it (and at a higher level). What do you need to do more of this year in order to become the kind of person who can drive significant growth?

Once you have your answers to those four questions, you have a road map for this year. Then it's just about execution.

Some of these you'll have to do on your own (like stop checking email first thing in the morning).

Some of these you might need a coach for (like developing a certain skill or ability).

Some of these you might need a counselor for (hey, we all have baggage).

Some of these will be mental changes you'll have to work on (like, stop playing small and start playing big).

Some of these you'll need to read books on or take course on or do research about.

But one thing is absolutely clear. If you want to ensure this coming year is better than this last year, you have to become a different person than you were last year. Remaining the same is not an option! Now, who do you need to become this year to drive the kinds of results you want?

Ted Federici

Don't Start Small and End Small

Fact: Most businesses never reach $1 million in annual sales. They start small and end small. While you can certainly create a great income with lower revenues, depending on your net profit, it's also true that staying small does not necessarily ensure that your business will survive.

There are no guarantees in business or in life! Every entrepreneur is faced with the risk that all his or her hard work and sacrifice will go belly-up. You have two choices for dealing with this uncertainty: shrink and survive, or survive through evolution and growth.

If you increase your annual revenues, you'll find you have more options. You'll be in a more likely position to ramp up your advertising or fund your own growth. There's also the old saying, "Revenue covers a multitude of sins," meaning that you don't have to have a perfect business to do well, as long as revenues are high and cash flow is healthy.

If times get tough and people aren't buying as much, you'll have your savings to weather the storm, your revenues will have room to decrease without putting you completely out of business, or you may have the cash on hand to get aggressive and attack your way out of the slump. Plus, you'll make more from the sale of your business, after all your hard work.

Whereas, if you stay small in order to keep things more manageable, it is often just a case study in shrinking back within the confines of your comfort zone. (Yes, I know, you're a fearless entrepreneur and nothing daunts you, but let's get real here.) Everyone has a comfort zone, and the fulfillment of dreams rarely happens within their limited boundaries. *You will have to grow* ahead of your business.

With the mindset of achieving and maintaining fast growth, here are some tips for forming a growth strategy of your own. Start with the most common ways for a smaller company to grow. Each of these involves some risk, effort, and uncertainty, though less than with other growth strategies. I suggest choosing and working on one of these at a time to stay focused and minimize the risks. These strategies are as follows:

1. Sell more to your existing customers. The growth strategy with the least risk is continuing to sell more of your existing products to your current customers. You can do this by offering upgrades, maintenance and

59

service packages, or finding new ways that your customers can use your product or service. If you can't figure out what else to sell to your customers, try this—*ask them*. Yes, it's really that simple.

2. Attract new customers. The next straightforward way to grow is to sell more of your product to adjacent markets—customers in different cities of states, or business buyers in related industries.

3. Find additional sales and marketing channels. This could mean making sales through new channels such as online transactions if you're a brick and mortar store or selling clothing at fairs and shows instead of strictly online. Or, you can advertise the same products through different lead generation channels, like pay-per-click, direct mail, etc.

4. Offer new products. Creating new products to offer existing customers is one sure-fire way to make more sales without having too much risk—compared to making new products for new customers. Think of new, related ways to meet their needs, or meet them better, or more easily. Try personalizing. Different colors. And, once again ask them what they want so you can give it to them!

5. Grow through acquisition. Another way to grow is to acquire other companies, though this is usually more capital-intensive. In addition, often-times mergers and acquisitions fail to deliver the full value predicted for them. Nevertheless, keep your eyes open for opportunities to buy competing businesses (especially if they're in a tough spot), or buying out one of your suppliers and even distributors to pass the savings through to your bottom line.

I hope you choose to grow your business versus staying small, and that you grow through one of these proven strategies. The horizon is constantly changing, and changing with it is a reliable way to stay ahead of the game and in a strong cash position.

CHAPTER 4:
MARKETING AND SALES

Increase Revenues

As you know I often think and we often talk about how to increase your revenues. I offer you four fundamental ways to increase your company's revenues and more importantly net profit. Don't discount any of these ideas. It's too easy to say "I'm already doing that," or "that won't work in *my* business." When, in fact, in most cases you can do a better job doing what you're doing, and/or creatively adapt the idea in your business. So have an open and creative mind, and see if some or all of these ideas can take your business to the next level. Here are the four methods:

1. Sell to and serve more people. This one is obvious—get more customers. Break it down further and look into all the possible *channels* by which you can advertise and reach new customers. Print, Internet, signs, trade shows, direct mail, and so on.

If you're like most, you may be advertising in some places, but not yet in others. Or, you may not be advertising at all. In some cases you ethically cannot advertise. The real issue is that you do not think of yourselves as marketers or salespersons and that, my friend, is exactly what you should be! You spend your time doing things that are demanded of you by your employees or customers instead of spending time to find tomorrow's revenues. There is another leadership issue to think about. You think sales are someone else's job! After all, you have assigned someone. Or worse, you know it is your job and you just find too many reasons not to get to it.

Why not start by changing your attitude? Sales are your job, plain and simple. If you don't do it, it won't happen. Obviously I am talking about your small business not IBM. After you decide to own it, try testing lots of different marketing channels to find new ones that can work for you. Start with the one that, as best you can tell, stands out as the one most likely to pay off (getting the most qualified people to contact you per dollar spent). Remember: the more marketing campaigns you try, the more likely it is you'll find the few that are solid gold. And these oftentimes become long-term assets, generating you profits month after month, year after year.

2. Increase your average order size. Restaurants know this one well. You in the service business know it well too. Get in the door, get the order, then increase it .Once someone has come into your sphere or on-line property, or calls you, your goal is to maximize their total order amount. In doing so, you should simultaneously maximize your revenues and completely fulfill the needs of your customer. Therefore, the person who has customer contact either in person or on the phone is your first point of sales. Tell them that. Maybe even incent them.

It doesn't have to be done obnoxiously. For example, when you're in a restaurant and the waiter suggests entrees, appetizers and/or asks if you want dessert, it's not seen as being pushy, and maximizes the restaurant's profits.

Another example of this you may have seen if you've rented a U-Haul or moving van. In those stores, you've probably noticed all the packing and moving supplies they sell. You could add to your customers' order sizes by finding out what accessories or related items they might need, and have them available. If you are a service professional such as architect, HVAC man or transportation expert, the same principles apply.

Online, you can see this done when you're adding items to your cart and going through "checkout." Often, other items are suggested at the last minute when you're in buying mode. Amazon.com is the master of suggesting products (think "Those who bought X also liked...") and it's no wonder they have one of the highest conversion rates among online stores.

3. Increase order frequency. How often do your customers need your product or service? Is it something totally out of your control, like a real estate client not needing to buy another house for several years? Or are there things within your control that can help customers to come in more often or purchase more often from you, like a restaurant inviting its customers in for specials on slow nights? Can you contact your customers in the slow season and offer specials?

Loyalty and reward programs can help make this happen. For example, most coffee shops will give you a card to punch each time you buy a coffee to get the 10th one free. If you have 7 of 10 punches already, you know you'll be a *little* more likely to choose that place over others to get your reward sooner.

Continuity income is another huge one. If you can offer any kind of product or service on a recurring, monthly basis...do it. A winery or liquor store could offer a wine-of-the-month club. Bakeries can offer weekly batches of cookies to local businesses for team meetings. The odds are that whatever you're offering, a certain percentage of people want it every month like clockwork and will pay accordingly for it.

4. Increase your monetization methods. Lastly, look for your business' byproducts that might be of value to someone else. An example of this is when sawmills and furniture manufacturers stopped throwing away the tons of sawdust accumulating on their floors, and began selling it to other businesses who could use it (such as for making "starter logs" for burning in your fireplace).

Another interesting example is a group of real estate investors who built a brand around their vanity number, 1-800-NO-AGENT, offering homeowners a chance to sell their house to them at a discount instead of listing it and waiting. They found they could sell the leads (those who responded but didn't' want to sell to them) to local real estate agents (who would contact them to see if they could represent them). They company ended up generating nearly as much revenue from selling "dead" leads as it did from their core business of "flipping" houses! I know these may be ideas you don't think apply; however I challenge you to change your attitude, think out of your comfort zone and try.

Competition

"Knowledge is power." This well-known saying is commonly attributed to Sir Francis Bacon, who was an English philosopher, statesman, scientist and author. In business, knowledge certainly is power. For example, if you knew where your market was heading, you would have a massive leg up on your competition.

So, how can you gain more knowledge to outsmart your competition? Learn from your customers, competitors, employees, community, consultants, mentors, and other business owners.

Marketing consultant Jay Abraham once said, "your customers are geniuses; they know exactly what they want." Steve Jobs said the direct opposite. Who is right? Both! Depends on where you are in your company and products. Life cycle. Because your customers know what they want, speak to them. And don't just speak to your current customers, but speak to your competitors' customers, too. Learn to listen deeply to your customers and to ask probing questions. And when you hear consistent feedback (and not just one customer saying something), take action.

Watch your competitors closely and learn from them. What do they seem to be doing well, and how can you better emulate them in this respect? What are they doing poorly that you can capitalize on? Importantly, don't just copy your competitors until you know that what they are doing works. For example, if a competitor starts offering a 25% off discount for new customers, don't copy them right away. Rather, wait and see what happens. If the competitor stops offering the discount quickly, then the promotion probably didn't work. Conversely, if the competitor is still offering the discount six months later, it probably did work. Only copy the competitor's "winners." Also try to figure out what competitors are saying about you. And, if criticism from a competitor gets back to you, don't be defensive or dismiss it casually. Rather, engage critically with it. The criticism may prove to be useful in a way that a customer cannot be because they do not know the details of the market. A competitor may be aware of your weaknesses in a way a friend or customer cannot be. So don't disregard negative feedback, but rather consider it carefully, and take corrective action as appropriate.

Oftentimes your employees have a lot more information than you do. They are the ones who are interacting with customers, and they are the ones that are building your products and providing your services. Speak to your employees and get their feedback, ideas, and suggestions. As an example, nearly all new innovation at Toyota comes from front-line employees. Encourage your employees to come up with ideas and give you feedback. They may also alert you to changes in the marketplace and customer behavior that you need to understand in order to adapt.

This is particularly true for local businesses. Find out what is going on in your community. For example, if your community is heavily involved in recycling, or if the local high school football team just won a championship, then you need to know about it since these are things your community cares about. Importantly, leverage this information. In these two examples, you could offer a sale related to the football team's victory. Or post signs explaining how your business recycles. These actions would position you as part of the community and cause customers to flock to your business.

The right coach and/or consultant will have lots of knowledge that you don't. They will have worked with other business owners and "been there, done that", that is, they will have seen challenges and overcome them already. Because you won't have to reinvent the wheel, these paid experts can allow you to make the right decisions, avoid mistakes, and grow more quickly. Plus, paid experts can give your business a reality check and keep you focused and accountable.

The right mentor serves a similar function as a paid coach and/or consultant in that they have experience, expertise and connections that allow you to avoid mistakes and grow your business more quickly. The challenge is finding the right mentor, and setting up the appropriate structure to get ongoing feedback (this naturally happens when you pay a coach or consultant).

In previous essays, I have mentioned the massive power of executive round table groups. These are groups of business owners who work together to grow everyone's business. They can be incredibly powerful since other members of the group may have already overcome the challenges you face, and thus can give you the answers you need. Likewise, in many cases, skills and knowledge that have taken other business owners months or years to learn can be transferred to you in minutes. In addition to knowledge, you'll quickly gain a support group that all shares the common goal of building a great company. Knowledge certainly is power. Leverage these ways to gain knowledge, and you will be able to outsmart and dominate your competition.

How to Answer Objections

In the process of business consulting and coaching, I've learned quite a few things that growing companies seem to have in common, no matter what industry they're in or what they sell. We all have cash flow to deal with, projects and teams to manage, and marketing campaigns to plan and carry out. Every business. But here's another common characteristic: pretty much all business owners face the four universal objections that their prospective customers have. They have time, need, money, and trust. What should you do about them? I suggest that you assume they have all four objections. Then, have a way to prevent each of them in advance through solid marketing and positioning and as they arise at the time of the sale.

Do this for every product or service, but start with the one that needs the most help (or would create the most revenues if improved). Come up with answers to these four objections—don't worry, I'll help—then have your whole sales process incorporate it.

Check each of the ads you're running to make sure they don't agitate one of these concerns, or show people in advance that it's not a concern. Check the language on your website and sales pages and make sure your salespeople have been trained in answering the objections.

Okay, enough explanations! Here are the four universal objections for which you should be prepared:

Objection #1: I'm too busy. This makes it hard to even get your foot in the door in the first place. At the advertisement level, people will skim over your ad and never commit to focusing on and reading it. You've got to show prospects fast that what you're offering is worth their time. The solution is to get their attention. Tease them with something, promise something, use memorable messages, and/or give prospects value up front.

Objection #2: Why do I need you? Particularly if prospects are not actively seeking the product or service you offer, you must show them why they need it. Show them what life can be like with your solution, how it solves a key need or pain.

Objection #3: I don't have the money. This objection comes up earlier than you'd think. It's partly because people and companies are both more cost-conscious these days, and partly from people's aversion to spending more money on something at all. "I don't have the money" is their excuse to bail before getting too invested in the decision-making process.

The solution here is to show prospects the value of what they are getting. Will your product or service enhance their lives, save them money in the future, position them to be more successful, etc.? Let them know the answer to this question! Another solution (which is not mutually exclusive) is to offer payment plans if possible to alleviate legitimate cost concerns.

Objection #4: I'm not sure I believe you. People are skeptical, and don't believe everything you advertise—and rightfully so. They want to know you're for real, and they want to see proof that your product or service does what you say.

Show them you're legitimate by letting them know your credentials, seeing your work, knowing your clientele or how long you've been in business, and also that you're honest, have integrity, and really care. One of the best ways to prove you can get results is showing testimonials from other customers. This is why "before and after" pictures are used in most weight loss commercials. This can be done with many products. Other things you can do to overcome skepticism include offering money back guarantees and simple return policies.

Getting new customers is one of the hardest things a business must do. By considering the objections prospective customer have, and preparing for them (via adjusting your marketing materials and training your sales team), you will more successfully attract new customers. This can and will give you a competitive advantage, and allow you to grow a successful company.

Ted Federici

Get and Keep New Customers

Smart marketers know that as much as 80% of their revenues come from repeat customers. Once you transform someone from prospect to customer and then give him or her a great experience, your next sale to that customer will be much easier. In fact, oftentimes the customer will initiate the next sale without any effort on your part.

The best way to get more sales from repeat customers is...make more sales to first-time customers! For instance, if your initial sale to a customer is $40, but the average customer will purchase four more times within the first year, then a new customer is actually worth $200 in the first year. Much more than the initial $40! Clearly, you want to attract as many new customers as possible (and take care of them so they keep purchasing from you).

To help you do this, below are three tips for attracting first-time customers. Since it's the most important sale you'll make, it pays to make your offer truly attention-getting and irresistible.

First-Time Customer Strategy #1: Give Them a Deal. Some companies go as far as to lose money on their first sale (known as a loss-leader), knowing they'll make it back with an immediate upsell, monthly service, or future sales. Your goal is *not* to make as much money as you can on the first sale. It's to make a first sale!

Of course, it's better if the first sale naturally leads to selling your next item or service. For example, I know a pressure washing company who will clean your house's exterior at cost the first time. But then it upsells 80% of these customers to their "twice yearly" plan — this is where it derives tons of profits. Restaurants offer specials, phone companies offer you deals if you switch providers, etc.—you know the drill. Give customers a powerful offer to which it's hard to say no, either in the form of a low price or incredible value for their money.

You see coupon offers and deal-of-the-day sites like Groupon offering $20 massages and other great deals all the time. This works in getting tons of new customers, but be careful. A lot of businesses have reported "The Groupon Effect," in which they will post a special, get a herd of penny-pinchers in the door that take advantage of the offer and then disappear to find the next deal at whoever's cheapest tomorrow. In other words, it can attract the wrong crowd and may not produce repeat business, which is the whole point of making a first sale.

Use these special offers carefully. One idea is to use direct mail. Doing so allows you to target the specific customers you want with your special offer.

First-Time Customer Strategy #2: Give Them an Experience. Think about how much money people spend on vacations, sports, dining, and entertainment. What do these all have in common? They're experiences that people want and are willing to pay for. You can try positioning your service as a personal experience. It's one thing to offer a massage, it's another to offer a "spa experience" with music, lights, nails, and a free facial. You can also plan and conduct group experiences like luncheons, parties, open houses, or tours. Or find a way to piggyback on existing events going on in your community, like parades, festivals, expos, etc.

These will take a little creativity, but remember that people are naturally drawn to fun times. Make it memorable and do it a few times per year. Look to Zappos.com as inspiration. Even though it sells a commodity (shoes), it provides a great experience through exceptional customer service. For many other businesses, providing a great experience is much easier than this.

First-Time Customer Strategy #3: Give Them Information. Every business needs to educate its customers, whether you charge for that education or not. I love it when my mechanic, Vinny, explains to me my car's problem, what caused it, how to fix it, and what it will cost. Sometimes we even go through options together, and I couldn't make a decision on the right one without getting the facts first. Providing education demonstrates that you're an expert, increases your trust, and gives you higher credibility in the customers' mind. It also gives you an easy segue into showing the benefits of what you're offering and how it will help.

Some lead generation methods tie in very well with education. For example, if you're trying to get blog posts ranked in the search engines, you'll need to write articles on topics of interest to your readers—like how to do something, the pros and cons of different products, etc. These posts will show your expertise and educate the reader.

You can do the same with videos. Simple, informative videos can get the attention of prospects and warm them up before contacting you. End each video with a special offer or a "call to action" that encourages the prospect to contact you.

To reiterate, consider how you can give first-time customers a deal, an experience, or the information they want/need. Use this to gain your first sales. Once you do, make sure you deliver quality, and then you'll be on track towards generating more repeat business than you can handle!

Gratitude as a Marketing Strategy

Some years ago, I began work with a business with awful accounts payable results and collection problems: almost all of its customers had open accounts and paid their bills ten to sixty days late (except those who didn't pay at all).

We quickly instituted a number of corrective measures, including tighter credit controls and policies, interest charges, a sequence of past-due notices, and collection calls. However, we also instituted a positive strategy. We started sending hand-signed thank you notes for prompt payment to anybody who did pay on time, those who were almost on time, and even late payers who responded to a past-due notice. Guess what happened? Those customers who received thank you notes became better paying customers.

I know a doctor who started a procedure of giving fresh, long-stemmed red roses to his women patients who showed up for their appointment on time, or paid their bills on time, or referred another patient. "Funny thing," he told me. "We no longer have patients missing appointments. Our collections have improved. Referrals are up. And, some guys are asking how they can get roses, too!"

Here are a few specific ideas you might adopt, as ways of saying thank you:

- Keep customers' birthdays on file and send cards and/or mail gifts.
- Send Thanksgiving cards or letters. Make it a habit to drop a personal thank-you note in the mail each day, to at least one customer.
- Send a gift certificate or discount certificate to a customer who makes an unusually large purchase.
- Host a "Customer Appreciation Event"—a Christmas party, a backyard barbecue. Have an occasional closed-to-the-public, preferred customer sale.
- Drop in personally on your best customers, with a surprise gift.

Just saying "thanks is a big step ahead of the competition today.

CHAPTER FIVE:
THE LEADERS

The Leadership Pyramid

As you move forward growing your business, remember core values: stay focused, manage by the financials, and bring your employees together as a team. The more they know about your goals, way of operating, and your attitude towards your customers, the more they will *intellectually, emotionally and physically invest in you!*
An effective leader follows these principles:

- Hire the right people
- Create the right culture
- Coach and inspire your people
- Establish accountability structures
- Develop the right performance incentives
- Fire people when needed (in the proper way)

To create the culture you want, give your organization a new premise to work in and be proud of. You are showing them, by incurring this expense, you have faith that the company will reach its goals.
You are the only obstacle to achieving your goal. Yes, you. Ask yourself these questions: Do my employees care as much about the business as I do? Are they psyched to come to work each day? Would the business thrive if you were off for a month? Are your employees better than your competition?
There is only one way to find out what your employees think: *Talk to them!*
Tell them your Vision of the company. Tell them what is in it for them when you succeed. Show them your goals. Show them how and where they impact the goals. Train and coach them.
Perhaps the most important of all is public recognition. Money is great, but recognition is far more powerful. When the boss says " I value you" publically to an employee, it resounds around the organization.
Similarly, kick ass when you need to. When the boss does not accept

incompetency, neither will the rest of the people. In a sentence: Be visible and communicate constantly.

Grunt Work and the Virtual Assistant

Outsourcing tasks and projects allows you to get more work done, more quickly, and for less money. It frees up your time to complete higher value-add tasks and otherwise grow your business. When outsourcing or delegating, a natural question arises as to when you should use several outsourced individuals, or one virtual assistant, or both, or hire someone.

Let me be clear: Hiring someone is the last resort! Do not create lasting overhead especially to handle tasks that perhaps should not be done at all or at least outsourced. This essay will help you better answer this question, and allow you to outsource more profitably.

Of the many types of providers to which you can outsource work, there's a certain amount of leverage you can achieve by hiring a virtual assistant trained to do many things.

Would you rather hire and manage different people for administrative tasks, research, editing and posting blog content, keyword research, contacting customers, scheduling appointments, SEO/getting backlinks, customer service, bookkeeping,...or, just hire one person to do them all?

Something I have found very helpful is to write up a big, long list of every task that currently must be performed for your business to operate. Make it a list of ongoing, necessary tasks (not project-related tasks—more on that later). Now go through the list and note which tasks are already handled by someone, which tasks could be done more inexpensively, which tasks you're currently doing yourself, and which tasks *should* be done but currently are not. Doing this will leave you with a list of ongoing tasks that should probably be completed by a virtual assistant.

What is a virtual assistant? A virtual assistant is a freelance service provider like any other, but who is more of a catch-all to handle numerous things for you (as opposed to an outsourced provider specializing in one thing, like design or computer programming).

Ideally, you can find one virtual assistant with previous experience doing everything you need done. If not, hire whoever can do the most and train them to do the rest. And/or for specialized projects, continue to hire individual outsourcers.

There are pros and cons to both virtual assistants and individual outsourced providers. One benefit of virtual assistants is that it's a lot easier to screen, hire, train and manage one virtual assistant for eight tasks than eight individual outsourcers for one task each. Conversely, the benefit of an individual outsourcer is generally that they are well-trained in their area(s) of expertise. If you need a writer for example, you will probably get better quality work from a professional writer than hiring (or training) a virtual assistant who does a variety of things including writing.

Another difference between virtual assistants and outsourced help is the length of time they work with you. Virtual assistants tend to be a longer, more ongoing commitment. Versus individual outsourcers who are often hired to complete just one task. Each of these scenarios has its benefits. Ongoing relationships cost more, but the virtual assistant often gets better with time as they learn more about you and your company. Individual outsourcers are only paid for the specific project they do, but there is more work to constantly find and educate them. With regards to cost, you can hire full-time virtual assistants in the Philippines for only $5 per hour, or $400/month full-time! So the cost might be very reasonable.

You may ask, What should I have my virtual assistant do first? The list of tasks you made above can also be used when posting a project to hire a virtual assistant. These core tasks become their job description. As you think of new tasks your assistant can perform for you, add them to the list and train them to do it when the time is right. You can't teach them everything all at once, so you've got to have a planned and orderly system for training your assistant. Number each of the tasks in the order in which you want to train them.

I recommend numbering only the top five at first so that you will stay focused. To number more is a waste of time, and your priorities might change in the meantime, anyway. When you're almost done with the first five, choose a new top 5 tasks to teach, with the current #5 becoming the new #1.

There are three methods you can use to prioritize what to teach your virtual assistant and when:

Based on frequency. Using this approach, the first things you would train your assistant to do are the ones they will be responsible to perform every day. This makes sense, because these tasks are needed most often, and they will begin to establish a daily routine. These tasks will become a habit, which will ensure they are done on time, every time. Once these are taught, you can then move on to items that are to be done weekly and then monthly. Think of training your virtual assistant in things that happen regularly as the foundation. Once it is laid, you can build upon it by adding other tasks that arise from time to time.

Based on time consumed. The first things you would teach your assistant to do using this approach are the ones that currently take *you* the most time to do. By doing this, you free up your time a lot faster. Some of these tasks take a long time to train; others will only require an hour or so. You may prefer getting these monkeys off your back sooner, and like this method better.

Based on importance. There are some things that each of us really needs to do, but we just can't seem to find the time to accomplish. You may wish to teach these to your assistant first in order to make sure they get done.

You may also decide on some combination of the above. Use your judgment, and don't put off things that should be trained just because they take a few hours to teach properly.

While outsourcing can certainly save you a ton of time, there is still some unavoidable work on your part to get it set up for success and to manage and coach your virtual assistant over time. So the point is...you have to put in the hours and pay the price in order to get top-notch results consistently. But would you spend one hour to save ten? Ten hours to save one hundred? I hope so. Taking the time to properly train and manage your virtual assistant and individual outsourcers is one of the best ROI's you'll ever see in business—but there is still an investment to make. I'm hammering this home because I see a lot of entrepreneurs hiring someone, throwing them into the work, and then getting busy again with other things, wishfully hoping that everything will just run on auto-pilot from the beginning. It won't.

How to Think Successfully

I just finished reading a biography of Amelia Earhart, an out-of-the-box thinker who saw barriers, figured out how to overcome them, and then did so!

"Never interrupt someone doing what you said couldn't be done." This quote from Amelia Earhart is one of my favorites, and I think it is especially applicable to entrepreneurs. Since most entrepreneurial achievements are ones that seemingly couldn't be done.

Take Google. Would you have thought that this startup, that initially faced heavy competition from other search engines like Yahoo, Alta Vista, Lycos, and others would eventually dominate the industry? Or how about Apple? Would you have bet in 2004 that Apple would develop sensational products and become the world's largest company based on market capitalization? And that from 2004 to 2011, the company's revenues would grow *eight* times?

Both of these feats, and virtually every other feat achieved by entrepreneurs and entrepreneurial companies, have seemingly been impossible. But, they were achieved. Which leads to the question of "why?" Why were these entrepreneurs able to achieve these amazing feats while most other fail?

From my work helping entrepreneurs start and grow their businesses for over a decade, and from reading countless books on success, I have identified five key reasons why entrepreneurs achieve success. And I expect that Amelia Earhart thought and did these things as well on her way to becoming a legend.

Surround yourself with winners. Success coach Jim Rohn said, "You are the average of the five people you hang around with most." It's true. If you hang out with losers, unfortunately you'll be a loser. But if you hang out with winners, you'll become a winner. Because winners have a different way of thinking. And winners (particularly other successful entrepreneurs with whom you should be spending time) have often already encountered and overcome the challenges you face in your business.

How do you surround yourself with winners? Meet them at networking events. Seek them out (e.g., successful local business owners and executives).

Ted Federici

Amelia Earhart also surrounded herself with winners. She was mentored and taught by famous air racer Frank Hawks and pioneering aviation teacher Anita Snook. She also spent significant amounts of time with ultra successful entrepreneur and book publisher George P. Putnam.

Identify your limiting beliefs and then overcome them. Limiting beliefs are beliefs that we hold either consciously or subconsciously that serve as obstacles to achieving and attracting what we want. For example, each year many schoolchildren are told by teachers that they "aren't smart" or "won't amount to much." As a result, these children often carry, throughout their lives, this extremely negative and limiting belief. They incorrectly believe, at either conscious and/or subconscious levels, that they can't achieve success, and as a result they don't.

This holds very true in business, and, as such, it is imperative that you both identify and overcome your limiting beliefs.

For example, do you hold any of the following limiting beliefs?

- I don't have enough time to become a successful entrepreneur.
- I can't start or grow my business since I don't have enough money.
- Failure is shameful, and if my venture fails, I will be shamed.
- I can't be a successful entrepreneur because I'm lacking certain educational degrees.
- I can't change or improve; I do things my way and that's who I am.

These false beliefs and "excuses" prevent many entrepreneurs from achieving greatness. So identify these beliefs and force yourself to expel them.

Accept the idea of failure. While you shouldn't dwell on the possibility of failure, you must accept it. If you don't, you may be striving in your business to prevent failure, rather than striving to achieve success. The latter will always help you achieve better results.

It turns out that actual failure is never as bad as we think it will be. Specifically, research shows that when people fear the worst and it happens, it's not as bad as they thought it would be, and they recover quickly. Many entrepreneurs have failed before achieving success. Milton Hershey, P.T. Barnum, Henry Ford and Walt Disney. All of these super-successful entrepreneurs failed big at one point in their careers and had to claim bankruptcy.

That's why I love this quote from Phil Knight, the co-founder and chairman of Nike, Inc.: "People only remember your last success." So, even if you've failed before, or fail again, as long as you end up on top, that's all people, will remember. A friend of mine sent me a quote recently: "One is not a failure no matter how many times your ventures fail; until one starts blaming others for the failures."

Dream positive. What you think about most often comes true. So you need to stay positive. For example, rather than thinking about what to do to prevent customers from leaving you, think about ways to better satisfy your customers and get them to tell all of their colleagues about you. At the end of the day, both of these thoughts are similar, but framing it in a positive light is proven to increase your chances of success.

Believe in yourself. The biggest barrier to your success can be thinking that what you are doing is not possible or that you are not smart enough to make it happen.

Consider this story as told by marketing consultant Dan Kennedy: "One of my clients, who made over $100 million in his business in its first three years, had gone broke several times before. Finally, after three years of remarkable success, he said, "Making $100 million is about the easiest thing I've ever done. Believing it could happen to me, or rather I could make it happen was the hard part that took 20 years."

You must believe in yourself if you want to succeed. You *can* do it. Simply stating that you can do it in front of a mirror every morning for 30 days will improve your belief in yourself. Maybe that sounds hokey to you, but it works, and if you really want to become a super-successful entrepreneur, it's worth doing.

Ted Federici

Play to Your Strengths

The Chinese have long held the Olympic gold medal in Ping-pong. At the 1984 Olympics, when they again captured the gold, the coach of the Chinese team was asked by a reporter, "Tell me about your team's daily training regimen." He replied, "We practice eight hours a day perfecting our strengths. Here is our philosophy: If you develop your strengths to the maximum, the strength becomes so great it overwhelms the weakness. Our winning player, you see, plays only his forehand. Even though he cannot play backhand and his competition knows he cannot play backhand, his forehand is so invincible that it cannot be beaten." Importantly, what the Chinese coach said is a proven leadership theory known as "Strengths-based Leadership Theory."

Strengths-based Leadership is a way of improving a company's success by developing the organization's strengths. The key to this proven philosophy is that people have a significantly higher ability to further improve on their strengths versus fixing their weaknesses. Makes sense doesn't it? Yet most entrepreneurs and leaders do the opposite—they focus on improving their and their employees' weaknesses. This leads to frustration and lack of high performance. Rather, you should be constantly improving your strengths, so, as the Chinese ping pong coach stated, your strengths are "so invincible that you cannot be beaten."

So, how do you implement this in your organization? Here are four principles:

1. List your organization's strengths. A strength is defined as the ability to exhibit near-perfect performance consistently in a given activity. Create a list of the strengths that you and your employees have.

2. Rank your organization's most important strengths. With your list of strengths, figure out which ones are core to the success of your organization. For example, strengths that allow you to produce a better product or service for your customers would be key as it can give you sustainable competitive advantage. Rank your key strengths.

3. Invest in further developing your employees' strengths. Invest time,

energy, and money (via training, education, etc.) in further developing your employees' top-ranked strengths so they get even better and you can dominate competition. Remember, just having a strength isn't good enough. Consider professional athletes. They all have great strengths. But the world's best professional athletes are the ones that constantly practice and improve on their strengths.

4. Outsource your weaknesses. To operate, every company needs to perform many tasks that may fall outside of their strengths. For example, a company that is incredible at making the best wines needs to do many other things. Such as answering incoming phone calls, shipping the wines (to distributors, retailers and customers), creating and maintaining a website, etc. Importantly, if their wine is that superior, then these other functions are far less important and do not require the company to have competitive advantage.

Such a firm should outsource these tasks to another firm who focuses on these functionalities (e.g., a web design firm, a trucking company, etc.). They could also consider hiring people who have strengths in these areas. However, in this case, they may also need to hire an operations manager to manage these hires so that they company head can continue to focus on their strength of creating the best wine.

In summary, great leaders do not create companies that are great at everything. Rather, they figure out their key organizational strengths and further develop the most important ones. This gives them lasting competitive advantage.

Setting Priorities at Work

Trap #1: Prioritization

Setting workplace priorities is by far the most common time management complaint I hear. It comes in two flavors: either the worker has problems juggling multiple projects and can't set his or her own priorities, or the boss has problems setting priorities for the employee. Often, the boss labels everything as equally urgent, leaving workers to throw up their hands in frustration and simply guess which project to focus on-which may cause drama and stress later on, if they guess wrong or the boss proves unreasonable.

Whether the failure to set priorities is the boss's or the worker's, the worker ends up scrambling and may soon fall prey to overwork and overwhelm (which represents another common time trap; see below).

The solution, while easy to state, may be difficult to accomplish: firmly ask your boss to prioritize your projects. Then ruthlessly triage your task list, focusing first on the items that truly matter. Prioritize everything else according to relative value.

Trap #2: Interruptions and Distractions

This timewaster consists of anything unscheduled but routine that disrupts an individual's focus and thereby damages productivity at work. Meetings and crises don't count; they have their own categories. I imagine you could fill up a whole page (or more) with a list of the various interruptions and distractions that impact your workplace productivity: coworkers who drop in at random intervals; ringing phones; noisy neighbors; and micromanaging bosses.

Communications issues, especially those involving email and phone calls, plague us all constantly, and represent almost a third of this category of complaints. Overcoming this particular trap requires a firm application of self-discipline. If something distracts or interrupts you, make the effort necessary to guard against it. If you have an executive assistant, have them guard access to you; otherwise, tighten your focus. Use ambient sound or music to block out noise. Turn off your email alerts and close your browser. Forward your calls to voicemail when you have no time for calls and respond a few times a day. Go somewhere quieter for a while or work from home one day a week.

Trap #3: Overwork/Overwhelm

This problem boils down to: "There's not enough time in the day to do everything!" Given the human need for rest (and sanity), workers can push themselves only so far within the unforgiving limitations of the 24-hour day. Time is a constraint no one can bargain with or stretch.

Take firm control of your time, jettisoning the unimportant tasks from your schedule, and maintaining an unremitting, tight focus. Examine each task and determine if you've been overdoing it; in other words, can your downstream user make do with less? If the task really belongs to someone else, give it to them. To the maximum extent possible, find ways to delegate tasks to others, and practice purposeful abandonment: if you run out of time for something of minor relevance, let it go. Stop seeing your task list as a "must do" list, instead viewing it as a "want to do" list.

These steps represent only the beginning of a valid prioritization effort, but taken together, they're big steps-and they can help you deal with the beast of overwhelm before it devours you.

Trap # 4. Lack of Self-Discipline

For some people, the biggest time management problem is actually a lack of self-discipline: i.e., not having the willpower to say no to distractions, or to stick tenaciously to the task at hand. Many people won't admit it, however. Many employees are unable to concentrate or attempt to multitask too much. Too often, they lose track of the projects they're juggling, which echoes prioritization and planning issues as well. Others have problems with setting or sticking to goals...and a few just can't seem to get anywhere on time.

To overcome these problems, fire up your willpower, crack the whip on yourself, and decide to concentrate on a task until complete. About a quarter of those with self-discipline problems see procrastination as a bigger issue than a simple lack of focus. Most often, they find themselves daunted by huge, complex projects. So in addition to applying tight focus to the problem, break it into smaller chunks you can handle more easily. Set milestones, buckle down, and get to work.

Trap # 5: Disorganization

Many workers accept a high level of chaos in their lives, and as a result find themselves stuck in the time trap of disorganization. Information constantly gets lost or misplaced.

Tracking action items, managing the boss (or subordinates), filing, planning, and overall project management sometimes overwhelms these workers, because they don't have a logical information processing system in place.

Learn to use your email software to its fullest, establish a logical, simple organizational system, and process every piece of information as it enters your life. Don't let it pile up, and never dither about what to do with an item-whether a piece of paper, an email, a voicemail, or any other bit of information that crosses your desk.

Always make time for planning. And occasionally, step back and look at the big picture, so you can see how everything is working. As necessary, take steps to fix what doesn't work, and be on the lookout for ways to improve efficiency.

Trap # 6. Scheduling

Do you have problems getting things done in the time you have? Common complaints include an inability to properly estimate how long specific tasks will take (a skill that comes with experience), and deciding where on one's calendar to place each task.

The second case requires thoughtful (and stringent) application of both task triage and prioritization, as well as a willingness to say no to new work when possible. You especially have to learn to let things go.

You can't get important things done when your calendar is burgeoning with unimportant meetings. Most of us prefer to do the easy, fun tasks first-an unproductive attitude at best. Instead, do the hard, high-significance things first. You can let go of the rest if time runs out.

Trap# 7: People Problems

Jean-Paul Sartre famously said, "Hell is other people" and yes indeed, your coworkers can present a variety of difficulties when it comes to getting your work done. As I've already discussed, many workplace distractions emanate from others. Who hasn't been annoyed by coworkers gossiping in the hall, or playing their music too loud?

Upper echelon workers often find that management duties represent their biggest time challenges; but those come with the job. Productivity at work suffers more when people act as roadblocks and bottlenecks. A few seem to do it on purpose, often from sheer cussedness.

Some don't care about your deadlines, so they don't get important information to you in a timely fashion. Others just can't seem to get anywhere on time, thereby wasting your time. And when a boss can't (or won't) make a decision, you might end up twiddling your thumbs until they do.

Some bottlenecks you can go around. Some you can break by stepping in to help, or at least by asking the blocker flat out what the hold-up is. Whatever the case, try to smooth the way so you can get the workflow process moving again. If you can't, then accept the situation as something you can't change and move on to something else.

Trap #8: Crises

The time trap of the unexpected runs neck-and-neck with people problems in my informal survey. In fact, most workplace crises arise from human behavior in one way or another. Bosses dump urgent projects on you at short notice, slow coworkers keep dragging their heels until you can barely meet your deadlines, human bottlenecks tie up resources, and everything suddenly comes due right now. We've all been there—and we'll all certainly be there again.

You can't do much when other people spin things into crisis, except react, which means you must remain perpetually flexible. Establish systems and processes in advance to handle the unexpected when it lifts its ugly head, including guidelines for each type of emergency you can imagine. When a crisis arises, practice SLLR: Stop, Look, Listen, and Respond. After you have a handle on the situation, spring into action.

You may have to triage your to-do list again, with some tasks moving down or off the list as a result. If you've already scheduled a little extra time into your schedule, let it take up the slack. Do all you can to address the new work while letting as few of your normal tasks go as possible- and get all the help you can while doing so.

Trap #9: Work/Life Balance

It may sometimes seem like your organization doesn't want you to have a life outside of work, considering everything they pile on you.

Workers tend to accept excessive hours as part of the background noise. Mostly, people just want a personal life, so they can pursue their hobbies, rest and relax, exercise, go to school, or (the #1 response) spend more time with their families. Again, the solution involves a strict adherence to self-discipline, ruthless task triage, and relentless prioritization, so you can make a big enough hole in your schedule to enjoy life outside of work.

Focus on being efficient and productive at work, so you can achieve maximum results in minimum time, leave the office earlier, (can you get down to 10 hours instead of 12?), and get a life.

Trap #10: Meetings

No organization can function without face time; so inevitably, meetings take up some portion of the average worker's daily schedule. In some organizations, they get out of hand, directly harming workplace productivity.

Finding enough time to actually fit in work when you regularly spend half the day in back-to-back meetings can be difficult. And before you accuse me of exaggeration, I do know people who've worked such jobs.

When meetings go bad, the problem, again, tends to be because of oblivious people. They go off on tangents, won't get to the point, or simply can't communicate well; whatever the case, they err by wasting everyone else's time.

Besides fighting this tendency in yourself, you can overcome the meeting trap by cutting down your commitments to meetings, going only to those you absolutely need to attend, and setting time limits you communicate to everyone as soon as you arrive. If you can, leave once you've made your contributions. If the meeting goes over the allotted time, politely excuse yourself, citing another meeting to attend.

And there you have it! That rounds out my list of ten time management traps, based on my years of experience working with people at all levels and helping people hone their workplace productivity. Most interrelate in a variety of ways, both obvious and subtle.

As I've mentioned repeatedly, the secret to overcoming these time traps will always be hard work and unremitting vigilance in the form of task triage, serious efforts at prioritization, and laser-like focus: simple and straightforward enough, if not especially easy!

Stay Away

There are certain four-letter words that have no business in business. Many, in fact, are bad for business—so bad that using them may determine whether you stay in business.

No, we're not talking about profanity here, that's a given. These are everyday words that really smart people eliminated from their vocabularies early on. Let me share some of the most offensive. I've even used them in sentences so you can see how to avoid some common mistakes.

Can't: As in "We can't do that" or "You can't expect us to meet that deadline." Your customers come to you because they think you can do what they ask. If you truly cannot produce what they're asking for, be honest but then help them find someone who can, even if it's your competition. They'll remember that you went the extra mile to make them happy.

Busy: "I'm too busy to do that now" or "I'll call you when I'm not so busy." The last thing your customers want to know is that they rank at the bottom of the food chain. It is acceptable to say that you will need a few days to do the job right, or that you'll knock off a few bucks in exchange for their patience. It is never okay to imply that they aren't as important as all your other customers.

Bore: "This project is such a bore" or "Don't bore me with the details." Unemployment is boring. Try to find something to love about every customer account you serve. An ingenious salesperson always will. Life is too short to be bored or boring.

Same: "We've done it the same way for years" or "Same old, same old." If you've been doing something the same way for years, it's a good sign you're doing it the wrong way. Maybe it's time to find a new and better way to do it. People change. Technologies change. Your customers aren't asking you to dye your hair purple and wear your kid's jeans. But their businesses change and they're looking to you to follow-or to lead. You should question why you're still doing things the same old way

Safe: "Let's play it safe." Safe is important in baseball, but in business you must be prepared to take some risks. The scary part about taking risks is that they don't always work. That said, I'd take a good calculated risk any day of the week over the boring, same, safe way. Sometimes it's risky not to take a risk. To triple your success ratio, sometimes you have to triple your failure ratio. Smart customers know this, too.

Rude: No example sentence needed here. There is never, ever, an excuse to be rude to a customer, coworker or stranger on the street. You're staking your name on your behavior, and you don't want your name to become a four-letter word.

Mean: Your lawyer should be mean. Your tennis serve might be mean. You can't afford to be mean. You are dealing with customers whose business and referrals will determine where your kids go to college and what kind of retirement you can look forward to. If that doesn't make you nice, I don't know what will.

Isn't: "That isn't our job." A salesperson's job description always includes every last chore that's required to satisfy the customer. You need to take your turn. That's how you become invaluable to customers. Never pass up the chance to do something new, just because you're too good. The farther up the ladder you climb, the farther down you can fall. It's important for your firm to have secure footing on each rung.

Fear: "I fear we may be moving too fast" or "My biggest fear is that we can't do this" only demonstrate one fact: you haven't done your homework. Common sense, thorough research and sound advice should allay your fears to a reasonable level. Knowing what is acceptable risk should help too. If your biggest fear is that rain will ruin an outdoor promotion, plan something inside. If you fear your suppliers will keep you from meeting a production deadline, find a more reliable supplier. Take charge.

Last: "Nice guys finish last." I consider myself a nice guy, and I hate to finish last. But I've had to lose a few times in order to win the next round.

Self-confidence

Self-confidence exercises are a way of building strength. Instead of focusing on physical strength, these exercises build character and self-respect.

For these self-confidence exercises, you will need a special journal. The first exercise is at the end of each day write down any event in which you receive positive feedback. If you get a well-deserved compliment from your boss, write it down. If your family expresses appreciation for something you've done, such as prepare a special meal or take the family on a picnic, add that to your journal as well. If your child tells you that you're the best mom or dad in the world, record that in your journal.

You can also include in your journal memories of past events that you handled well. It is human nature to remember our failures. If you dwell on the things you have done wrong in your life, your self-confidence will decrease. Instead, remind yourself often of all the things you have done right in your life, both large and small.

Another exercise is to challenge yourself to take a risk to confront a situation you've been avoiding. For example, if you have been avoiding social situations because you tend to be awkward and shy, challenge yourself to attend one event and meet one person. Or if you've been avoiding trying to change jobs because you don't handle interviews well, make the effort to schedule one interview. Be sure to include your own observations of your progress. If you deal with a stressful event in a positive or successful way, write it down.

There is no room for negativity in this journal. The purpose of these self-confidence exercises is to get in the habit of expressing praise toward your self. Each day, the goal is to record at least one thing you did right. If you don't have a particular event to write down, fill in the blanks of the following types of sentences:

- The thing I do best is…
- Something I have accomplished is…
- One of my best character traits is…
- I am proud of myself for…
- I am working to improve…

Give yourself a small amount of time for meditation and reflection. In this quiet time, picture yourself succeeding at the type of activity that causes you self-doubt. Picture yourself as a *successful public speaker* for example, or handling yourself at ease in a social setting.

Self-confidence exercises can also include affirmations. *Make positive statement to yourself first thing in the morning, before the concerns of the day have set in.* Several times a day, continue to repeat statements such as the following:

- I am confident in my ability to handle whatever will come up today
- I am improving every day
- I deserve to be happy and successful

These self-confidence exercises are small ways you can begin to work on your sense of self-worth each and every day. You will be surprised at how quickly this will make a difference in your life.

Staying Focused

You know that one aspect of leading and managing your business is the need to stay focused. More than ever, modern workers are bedeviled by distractions and interruptions that pull us away from the key activities of our jobs. If it's not your noisy office-mates, it's the siren song of the Internet, or an over-fascination with email. Therefore, it's imperative that you learn to trim your activities down to the few things that are truly important, so you can actually get your job done.

Proper focus requires discipline and mastery to achieve, like any other skill. In this essay, I'll help you get started in your quest to wield your focus like a blade, stripping away the things that keep you from getting your work done on time and under budget.

Let's start with one of the worse culprits: your subconscious.

Eliminating self-sabotage. If you're like most people, many of the distractions you face when trying to focus are self-imposed. Some are activities that you consciously engage in, like chatting over the phone without purpose, or getting up too often for a cup of coffee, without realizing that they're slowing you down and blunting your focus. Some, however, are percolating along under the surface, all but invisible-but damaging nonetheless.

There are two other subconscious drivers: perfectionism and procrastination. Perfectionism is based on the admirable desire to do the very best job possible; but when taken to extremes, it can distract you from getting the job done. Trying to work out every little detail and plan for every possible contingency ahead of time can result in time-wasting paralysis. Instead, once you've made a decision to do something, get started and work through the details as they arise.

Procrastination is simply dragging your feet because you don't want to do something. In the final analysis, your reasons for doing so don't matter; if you procrastinate for any reason, the result is lost productivity. The solution is to force yourself to work: visualize what you need to do, break it down into smaller tasks that are easier to handle, and then buckle down and get it done. Easier said than done, perhaps, but it's just as necessary to push through procrastination as it is to jettison perfectionism.

Ted Federici

One self-sabotage topic I haven't previously discussed is negative self-talk. Each of us goes through life constantly thinking about and internally commenting on the situations we encounter. This "self-talk" helps us manage our reactions and decide what to do next. Unfortunately, self-talk can be self-defeating. If you convince yourself that something's too difficult or that there's no point in trying, you throw roadblocks in the path of productivity. Negative self-talk is a prime component of procrastination, and can also contribute to perfectionism-for example, if you keep telling yourself you've got to do something just right or else.

You've got to get a handle on negative self-talk before it leads you into the slough of depression and ruins your productivity. The best thing to do is to dispute it all the way down the line. First, do a reality check: are your facts straight? What evidence do you have for your negativity? Are you jumping to conclusions? Next, put it all in perspective. Challenge your self-talk:

- Is the situation *really* as bad as it seems?
- If so, what's the worst thing that could happen?
- How about the best thing?
- What's most likely to occur?
- How would I perceive this situation if I were in a positive mood?

It's difficult to eliminate self-sabotage in any of its forms, since many of us tend to be our own worst critics. But in order to be productive, you have to be realistic and ruthless about facing down your subconscious.

The mistake of multitasking. Have you ever heard the saying, "Energy flows where attention goes"? That may sound a bit glib, but it's spot on. For biological reasons, most of us can absorb and integrate only so much input at once; we literally have a limited amount of attention that we can pay out.

This is why multitasking doesn't work very well, despite all our attempts to prove otherwise. You can't really develop a productive focus when you're trying to do more than one important thing at once. Yes, you can probably walk and chew gum at the same time, because those tasks are so simple that they tend to fade into the background. This isn't the case for high-level tasks requiring constant processing of new infor-

93

mation.

Consider cell phones and cars. Although most of us do it, we know it's foolish to talk on the phone and try to drive at the same time. Both tasks require such a high investment of cognitive resources that they detract from each other, causing us to do one or the other poorly—or more likely, both. The high number of phone-related car accidents is proof enough of this. So imagine how ineffective it is to simultaneously try to work on a report, chat, listen to music through ear phones, check the CNN website, and steal a second here and there to check your email. There's never an opportunity to drop into the kind of productive trance that gets the job done efficiently. *And above all: stop texting constantly, especially while driving!*

Multitasking isn't quite as subtle a form of self-sabotage as negative self-talk or procrastination, but you're still hurting yourself when you practice it. Learn to concentrate on one thing at a time, because attention is meant to be undivided. You can't afford to distract yourself, especially when you already have to deal with distractions from others.

Limiting external distractions and interruptions. A recent study concluded that 28% of the average knowledge worker's day is spent dealing with unnecessary interruptions, and then subsequently recapturing focus. That's outrageous! Clearly, you need to root out every source of interruption you can, and take steps to block other distractions as well.

Basically, this involves cutting yourself off from the outside world for *focused periods of time.* Other people aren't necessarily aware of your need for quiet, uninterrupted workflow, and many just don't care. If you've ever worked in an open-plan office, then you've probably been forced to listen to co-workers chattering about inconsequential matters outside your cubicle. Others will call or pop in unannounced. People get caught up in their own concerns and forget to be considerate, hurting your productivity in the process.

It's easy to insulate yourself if you're in upper management and have an office staff to filter out the inconsequential. But some of us don't even have the luxury of having an office door to close. Even so, you can arrange your workspace so you're not constantly derailed by interruptions and distractions.

If you can't completely shut yourself off, you still have options. First, you can try moving away from the worst disturbances. This may involve relocating permanently to a distant office or cube, or simply taking your laptop to the break room or to a bench outdoors, where you can work for a while in peace.

Otherwise, find a way to signal when you need to be left alone, and communicate it to your co-workers. For example, don't ask "How are you?" as you pass each other in the hall if you don't have time to hear the answer. Instead, say "Nice to see you," or just "Hi," and keep going. Whether you move or stay in place, you'll need to minimize noise distractions.

Finally, if your office uses shared scheduling software like Microsoft Outlook, you can also create a virtual "blackout" period by blocking out distraction-free periods on your schedule. That way, anyone who looks will know that you're unavailable, and they won't try to schedule your time for meetings and other interruptions.

Tackle the modern scourge of electronics. The "electronic leash" of email, smart phones, cell phones, and the like can disrupt your workflow, shatter your productivity, and hinder your focus. In order to avoid this self-inflicted ADHD, you've got to do right by yourself and come to your senses. These are tools, and you need to treat them as such—not as demanding little bosses constantly crying out for your attention. Why should you let them be in charge of you? Who's really the tool here?

The solution to electronic overwhelm is simple: when you're trying to concentrate, turn off and tune out. Kill the incoming message alerts on your email, chat clients, and social media. Let those phone calls roll over to voice mail. Sure, most of us need to stay in touch in order to get our jobs done, but who says you have to answer every message as soon as it comes in? There's very little that you have to attend to instantly.

Rather than allow yourself to be distracted and interrupted-which is exactly what you're doing when you stay constantly connected-set aside blocks of time when you can receive and answer your messages all at once, be they email or telephone. You can do it twice a day for half an hour at a time, once in the morning and once in the evening. That way, you can focus on getting your professional interactions taken care of all at once, without letting them defocus you throughout the day.

Be wary of socializing. The upshot of all this strenuous effort to head off distraction may be that you get labeled as unfriendly or distant. Well, so be it. If you're consistently productive, you can't listen to the critics.

Admittedly, social interaction is necessary to ensure the smooth functioning of any organization, but there's a time and a place for it. You have lunchtime, breaks, and the "twilight time" before and after work to rub elbows and be friendly with your co-workers. You can get to know them better when you're involved in team-building exercises, or take the time to do so offline, away from work. You can still be nice and get more than your share of work done.

The workday is for working; the rest of your life is for socializing and taking care of yourself and your family. The more you keep that in mind, the more you can keep your professional and social lives from bleeding over into each other-the better off you'll be.

The metacognitive edge. Metacognition, literally "thinking about thinking," is an excellent defense against distraction. How does it work? Simply enough: you implement strategies in which you use your knowledge about the way you think to shape your behavior. No one knows you as well as you do; if you'll just be honest about that knowledge and use it to your advantage, you can become more self-regulated and less distracted by the unimportant.

Learning to focus properly requires more self-reliance, and thus more metacognitive effort, than most workplace tasks; that's a given, so just accept it and move on. No matter how sloppy a thinker you believe you are, you can force yourself to focus if you're willing to apply self-discipline, stop sabotaging your own efforts, organize your workplace and work-life, and put your tools in their place. You constantly have to be on the ball, thinking about what it takes to narrow your focus to the few things that really count, and putting what you discover into play.

Yes, it's painful; and yes, it may be quite a while before you completely master your focus. But it's worth the effort.

The Inner Game

My new hip has caused me to rethink the sport I love most, tennis. I will not be playing singles which is no great loss to the game. So I am going inside to reinvent what I will do to stay active. It can be most anything that has a low impact effect on the body. What catches my attention is the thought, "Go inside." Some say if do not go within, you will go without. I say that all success comes from within.

There is an inner game of building your business, and I believe that it is simply all-important. "The inner game" is a term for a classic idea explained many different times, many different ways by virtually every success educator, and even philosophers.

For example, in the book *Think and Grow Rich*, Napoleon Hill reveals a profound insight, "thoughts are things." Dennis Waitley has worked with U.S. astronauts and Olympic athletes on their inner games. Author Tim Galloway explores the ideas of his books, *The Inner Game of Golf, The Inner Game of Tennis,* and *The Inner Game of Selling.*

Interestingly, there is a never-ending connection between the inner game in sport and the inner game in business, allowing experts like Waitley, Galloway, ex-quarterback Fran Tarkenton and golfer Arnold Palmer, among others, to move back and forth between expounding on success techniques in the athletic and business worlds.

In all cases, these people speak much more about attitudes than aptitudes, for a good reason. Surveys, studies and research, I have seen, consistently reaffirm that 85% of your success will depend on attitudinal factors, 15% on aptitude. Yet in your formal education and in most continuing education, the emphasis is on the opposite—15% on attitude, 85% on aptitude.

Certainly technical knowledge and skills are important. In your profession, you must deliver excellence based on your staying up to date in techniques, products, materials and ideas. However, such excellence alone will never build a successful, growing, profitable business. The excellence that will is an excellence created and sustained in your own mind. This is the most difficult, least tangible aspect of building your business that we'll ever talk about, but it is also probably the most important.

Yeah, but what is it? So what is the inner game? The way I see it, the

inner game can be broken down into four major components: self-esteem, self-image, self-confidence, and self-discipline.
In these four areas, quality is a necessary foundation to personal and professional success.

Self-esteem is essentially your feelings of worth. How much success do you deserve? How much money should you make? How much is your time worth? Here, briefly, are seven ideas for strengthening self-esteem:

- Establish worthwhile, meaningful goals and values.
- Take massive action to get your own financial house in order if it isn't now. Reduce debt, bring expenses under income, and invest every single month.
- Give yourself recognition for each and every accomplishment.
- Manage your time productively. Procrastination and disorganization rob many people of their self-esteem.
- Associate with positive-minded, happy people who encourage and motivate you. Don't hang out with folks who are negative, unhappy, critical or jealous.
- Continually acquire new know-how in you profession and in the areas of business, sales and communication.
- Regularly invest in improving your office and home environments, tools and equipment, wardrobe and other external things that impact on your attitudes.

Self-image is how you see yourself; it's who you think you are. Your self-image is controlled mostly by self-imposed limits. Very few people ever perform beyond those self-imposed limits. I call the concept "creating our own reality."

A salesman whose father never earned more than $25,000 a year in his life may well see himself as a $25,000 a year guy. And he will subconsciously screw up the opportunities to earn more that come his way.

In the financial area, there is a controversial behavioral concept called the money rejection syndrome, and I am convinced that such a thing exists. One man I read about, who made over $100 million in his business in its first three years from scratch, had gone broke in business several times before. After the three years of remarkable success, he said, "Making $100 million is about the easiest thing I've ever done. Believing it could happen to me was the hard part that took 20 years."

Your self-image was created and is sustained through self-talk, the use of affirmations—and that is also the method you can use to alter and modify your self-image, literally as you wish.

I call the process creating your own reality because most people who set goals set only "to get" and "to have" goals; they fail to set "to be" goals. I encourage you to balance your approach to goal setting by including some self-image modification.

Self-disciple, the fourth component of the inner game, is quite possibly the most important. Most people do not associate lack of discipline with lack of success. They think of failure as one earth-shattering event, such as a company going out of business or a home being foreclosed on, or a job loss.

Failure is rarely the result of some isolated event; rather, it is a consequence of a long list of accumulated little failures, which happen as a result of too little discipline. I agree. I find that most people understandably tend to look everywhere but in the mirror for the sources of their failures as well as the victories.

I'm here to tell you it's not the town you're in, not your location, not the economy, not the weather, not your competitors—it's your own discipline that makes the difference between excellence or mediocrity, between getting by or getting rich.

It's interesting to observe professionals. I often say to my associates in coaching, "Let me watch the professional's behavior before, during, and after the seminar, and I'll guess his annual income within a few thousand dollars." It's actually pretty easy to do.

I'd encourage you to take the self-discipline challenge very seriously. Select those areas that you know are your weakest links—timely paperwork, punctuality, daily self-improvement study, being happy and enthusiastic first thing in the morning, whatever your personal stumbling blocks are—and apply new, tough, demanding disciplines to yourself in those areas. You'll find that success in these particular areas of your day-to-day life will roll over into greater success in all parts of you life.

For example, let's look at the ultimate game players—professional team sports players. A pro ball player knows that every single moment of his on-the-job performance is recorded on film, to be replayed and reviewed later in stop-action slow motion, for critique by his superiors and co-workers. If your day was filmed and reviewed, how would you feel during the replay? Of course, the professional football players who have to put up with this sort of thing are highly paid.

Yes, the inner game stuff is tough. If being a big success were easy, everybody would be one. You've got to decide what you really want to be, do, have, accomplish—and decide whether or not you're willing to adhere to the disciplines necessary to get it.

Ted Federici

The Leadership Phenomena

When I think about the great entrepreneurs of our time like Steve Jobs, Bill Gates, and Richard Branson, I not only admire the companies they built, but their leadership skills. Even the best idea or the smartest individual can't evolve into a massively successful company without leadership. I often say, "Leaders lead people and managers mange process." Both are necessary skills but one need be aware of what is needed and when. Below I will explain the difference between leadership and management, and steps you may take to improve your leadership skills.

Leadership is future-oriented and determines what the company's desired future should be and what strategy to take to get it all done. On the other hand, management focuses on getting things done in the present through the wise use of systems, people, and resources. Leadership skills tend to be more intuitive, "big picture," and holistic. Managerial thinking tends to be more analytical, detailed, and logical. Both can be creative, but management thinking is definitely more process-oriented.

So how can someone become a better leader?

There are several areas of leadership for which each of us has some degree of skill. Take an analysis of yourself and where you stand on each of them below. While this can be a real eye-opener, doing this can let you know where improvement is most needed. It might just be the thing that is holding you back without you knowing it!

As I mentioned before, leaders have the ability to see the big picture and devise an effective path to make that vision come true. As a leader, you have the vantage point of looking at your entire business or any of its parts—sales, marketing, accounting, management, etc. You can look for opportunities or accept the need for change and create a vision in your mind of what could be. The clearer you are about what you want and what specific results are required, the easier it is to map an appropriate strategy that will get you there.

Leaders create the core values and philosophy of the business, grounded in their own values and passion. It's up to you to be consistent with regards to your company's values, so that it becomes "the way we do it" in your business.

For example, Zappos CEO Tony Hsieh attributes much of his com-

pany's success to the 10 core values he helped establish:

- Deliver WOW Through Service
- Embrace and Drive Change
- Create Fun and A Little Weirdness
- Be Adventurous, Creative, and Open-minded
- Pursue Growth and Learning
- Build Open and Honest Relationships With Communication
- Build a Positive Team and Family Spirit
- Do More With Less
- Be Passionate and Determined
- Be Humble

Leaders are committed. You must be willing to make sacrifices to achieve success. And you must be persistent and passionate to see things through to completion even with setbacks along the way. No one is going to be more committed to the success of your business than you, and your commitment will inspire those who work for you.

And lastly, leaders are influencers. As you frequently and powerfully communicate what your vision and strategy are, others will catch your spirit as well and see what you see. It can often be difficult to help other people to "get it," so as a leader you have to tailor your message to get through to them.

The funny thing about leadership is that it's the thing that most of us need to work on but we are perhaps the least aware of. After all, you don't know what you don't know. Where do *you* stand?

To help you, here are three simple steps to boost your leadership skills.

First, take an inventory of yourself and your skills in each of the areas in bold above. Specifically, ask the following questions:

- Seeing the Future: Do you have a clear vision of your company's future? Do your employees know this vision?
- Values: What are the values you live by and that your company needs to follow. Do your employees know these values?
- Commitment: How committed are you to the success of your

business? What would you forego in order to achieve that success (would you risk everything? give up watching TV? etc.)? Do you always follow through on company projects to completion?

- Influence: How much have you been able to influence employees and others? Have 100% bought into your vision? Do they come to work with "fire in their bellies"?

Not only should you answer these questions yourself, but ask someone you trust (including key employees) to give you their thoughts as well so you get a second point of view.

Next, determine where you are lacking and see how it has impacted your business. Specifically, are you happy with your answers to the above questions? If not, what might be the result if you don't change? What could be the result if you do change? Commit yourself to focusing on the area(s) in which you need improvement.

Finally, map out a plan for how you can improve in that area. Choose activities that will help you to practice that skill, and schedule them.

For example, if you feel like your vision for your business still isn't clear enough and needs some work, you might hold periodic vision meetings, attend conferences where you can scan for upcoming opportunities, or use some creative imagination techniques to explore possibilities in your mind.

Commit now to making your leadership skills an area of focus this year. With steady attention and effort, you'll find that you get results and realize your dreams more easily and quickly, and with a lot less confusion and spinning your wheels.

The Opposite of Steve Jobs

In an interview on his blog, billionaire and founders of the Virgin companies Sir Richard Branson said the following about Steve Jobs: "I admired Steve Jobs, although he was completely different from me. He used to shout at employees that made mistakes. He did not delegate much, and broke all the rules I believe in. Somehow it worked for him. Apple is one the best brands in the world." Branson, on the other hand, delegates a ton; how else could he manage nearly 50 companies at once?

Now, I'm not saying that Jobs' management style was any better than Branson's or vice versa. But clearly, even Jobs delegated a lot of business activities. For instance, Jobs clearly didn't do Apple's bookkeeping. Both Branson and Jobs are considered masters at delegating activities. That allowed them to focus on the highest value uses of their time to building their companies.

But a natural question arises for entrepreneurs with regards to delegating. And that is: what should I delegate or outsource? (From a definition standpoint, I consider "delegating" to be giving a task to someone else within your organization and "outsourcing" to be giving a task to someone outside your organization.) This question is particularly acute when you are an earlier stage entrepreneur with limited resources (versus Apple and Virgin who are billion dollar companies).

If you look at your business, there is probably a very long list of activities you could delegate, or rather (particularly if your company is relatively small) outsource.

For example, you might outsource activities related to: generating new leads, computer and IT infrastructure, bookkeeping, or new product or service development.

In addition to outsourcing tasks like these, you may simply choose to outsource tasks that are just plain annoying or take up a lot of your time. But, once again, if you're working with a limited budget, you will have to make some difficult decisions about what to outsource, and what to outsource now versus later.

Preparing to outsource. Even if you had unlimited funds, you would still want to prioritize what you outsource and when. This is because each task, role, or responsibility you give to someone else requires work. There is time required to plan the task, find and train the individual, and support or coach them among others.

For example, if you want to hire someone to call local businesses and set appointments for you, you would need to:

- Develop a general game plan of whom to call, how many people, what times of day, and for what purpose.
- Create a list of people to call, or develop parameters for the individual to use to develop their own list.
- Write a script the individual should follow when making calls.
- Create a list of the most frequently asked questions or concerns, to orient the individual on your product or service and what you can do for customers.

As you can see, simply preparing to outsource a task takes times, so you can't outsource everything.

What not to outsource: leads and new work generation. Since the biggest challenge of most businesses is not having enough leads and new business no matter how great your product or service, lead generation is probably one of the first things I would hold onto and work if you want to make more money. If you cannot do this yourself, then have the person who does it report directly to you and have a regular schedule of "How are we doing" meetings.

Task type 1: Fulfilling the business you generate. Once you generate leads and convert them into clients, you need to fulfill the orders. Particularly in service businesses, fulfillment often becomes a bottleneck; especially if you need to perform the work yourself. This typically results in a "feast or famine" cycle. That is, once you close a new client you are in "feast" mode from the money the new client brings in. But then, you spend all your time fulfilling the client, and when the work ends you are in famine mode. Specifically, because while fulfilling you didn't spend time on additional lead generation, once the client job ends, you are left without enough revenues and searching for new clients.

Consider putting someone in place to handle all the new business to generate. If not, you'll likely find your lead generation to be sporadic and less effective, or your customers not getting the quality of service they deserve.

Task type 2: Other ongoing, repetitive tasks. There are many tasks your business needs to perform over and over again—like bookkeeping, filing, creating reports, compiling data and contact lists into spreadsheets, researching vendors, etc. Your job is to grow your business by initiating new projects, not taking care of business as usual. So you need to outsource these administrative tasks.

Task type 3: Your most painful tasks. Each of us has our favorite tasks and our most dreaded tasks. And each of us has strengths and weaknesses. Ideally, you should perform the tasks which 1) you like, 2) which leverage your strengths, and 3) which have the most value to your organization. And certainly, if a task doesn't meet any of these three criteria, you must outsource it immediately.

The exception to this (and a warning) is when there is a skill or competency that you really do need to improve in order to be a successful business owner. Decision-making, planning, building a team, and other leadership responsibilities are not always fun, but critical to perform yourself (or with a co-founder or management team if necessary).

Action plan to get started. With these thoughts in mind, create a list of tasks that you are doing right now that aren't the highest value uses of your time. Also include tasks you aren't doing (e.g., lead generation tactics), but should in order to boost revenues and profits. I realize there often seems to be a chicken-and-egg issue, which is that you need money to outsource projects, but if you spend your time doing those projects yourself, you won't generate enough revenues or profits to pay for an outsourced person.

The answer is to take the leap. Go ahead and outsource a task or two. You will inevitably find you can generate more revenues and profits with the time you gain from outsourcing. You will eventually start outsourcing (and delegating) more and grow a thriving company. Make a quick list of the 5-10 activities you should outsource (either because they are a pain, you are not doing but need to do them, or they are low-level repetitive tasks). And then find someone to which you can outsource them.

Advice on How to Negotiate

Never accept any proposal immediately, no matter how good it sounds.

Never negotiate with yourself. You'll furnish the other side with ammunition they might never have gotten themselves. Don't raise a bid or lower an offer without first getting a response.

Never cut a deal with someone who has to "go back and get the boss' approval." That gives the other side two bites of the apple to your one. They can take any deal you are willing to make and renegotiate it.

If you can't say yes, it's no. Just because a deal can be done, doesn't mean it should be done. No one ever went broke saying "no" too often.

Just because it may look nonnegotiable, doesn't mean it is. Take that beautifully printed "standard contract" you've just been handed. Many a smart negotiator has been able to name a term and gets away with it by making it appear to be chiseled in granite, when they will deal if their bluff is called.

Do your homework before you deal. Learn as much as you can about the other side. Instincts are no match for information.

Rehearse. Practice. Get someone to play the other side. Then switch roles. Instincts are no match for preparation.

Beware the late dealer. Feigning indifference or casually disregarding timetables is often just a negotiator's way of trying to make you believe he/she doesn't care if you make the deal or not.

Be nice, but if you can't be nice, go away and let someone else do the deal. You'll blow it. A deal can always be made when both parties see their own benefit in making it.

A dream is a bargain no matter what you pay for it. Set the scene. Tell the tale. Generate excitement. Help the other side visualize the benefits, and they'll sell themselves.

Don't discuss your business where others can overhear it. Almost as many deals have gone down in elevators as elevators have gone down.

Watch the game films. Top players in any game, including negotiating, debrief themselves immediately after every major session. They always keep a book on themselves and the other side.

No one is going to show you their hole card. You have to figure out what they really want. Clue: Since the given reason is never the real reason, you can eliminate the given reason.

Always let the other side talk first. Their first offer could surprise you and be better than you ever expected.

FedEx Criteria to Identify Potential Leaders

According to FedEx, its best leaders share nine personal attributes—which the company defines with remarkable specificity. FedEx also has a system for rating aspiring leaders on whether they possess these attributes. How do you rate? Judge yourself against these edited descriptions of the nine faces of leadership at FedEx.

Charisma. Instills faith, respect, and trust. Has a special gift of seeing what others need to consider. Conveys a strong sense of mission.

Individual consideration. Coaches, advises, and teaches people who need it. Actively listens and gives indications of listening. Gives newcomers a lot of help.

Intellectual stimulation. Gets others to use reasoning and evidence, rather than unsupported opinion. Enables others to think about old problems in new ways. Communicates in a way that forces others to rethink ideas that they had never questioned before.

Courage. Willing to stand up for ideas even if they are unpopular. Does not give in to pressure or to others' opinions in order to avoid confrontation. Will do what's right for the company and for employees even if it causes personal hardship.

Dependability. Follows through and keeps commitments. Takes responsibility for actions and accepts responsibility for mistakes. Works well independently of the boss.

Flexibility. Functions effectively in changing environments. When a lot of issues hit at once, handles more than one problem at a time. Changes course when the situation warrants it.

Integrity. Does what is morally and ethically right. Does not abuse management privileges. Is a consistent role model.

Judgment. Reaches sound and objective evaluations of alternative courses of action through logic, analysis, and comparison. Puts facts together rationally and realistically. Uses past experience and information to bring perspective to present decisions.

Respect for others. Honors and does not belittle the opinions or work of other people, regardless of their status or position.

Ted Federici

How to Use Media

There are many forms of marketing which help entrepreneurs and small business owners get new customers. Referrals are perhaps the most powerful. I mean, what's more powerful than your customers urging their friends, family and/or colleagues to also buy your product or service? The second most powerful is publicity. If a prospective customer learns about you in most media sources, you gain credibility. And this prompts them to seek you out and buy from you.

There are many ways of getting publicity for yourself and your business. And when you do get it, there are several varieties. For example, a journalist may give you a simple quote in their article. Or, they may quote you several times or attribute the entire theme of their article to you. Or, in the best case, they write an article solely about you, your company and/or your product or service. The point is this—the more the article talks about you, the more likely the reader will seek you out after reading it.

One concern entrepreneurs and small business owners may have when getting publicity is what the journalist will say about you. Virtually all the time, the journalist will position your company in a positive light. But even if they don't, the saying "there's no such thing as bad publicity" is generally true. Importantly, there is one way to accomplish both the goals mentioned above: getting publicity (particularly articles) that fully discusses you and your company *and* gaining 100% control of what the article says about you. And that way is to write the article yourself.

Why articles?
Articles are a professional way to get the word out about your company without advertising, because they have educational value. They are an "under-the-radar" way to get positioned in front of people. *Here is the trick: send the articles to local community news papers not necessarily the biggies!*

What should you write about in your article?
Think of something you've learned in your line of work that your customers or prospective customers would want to know more about. Simply write out a one-page "how-to" article teaching the reader, or pre-

senting facts (and even debunking myths).

Where should you send your article?
Send your articles to relevant newspapers, magazines, trade journals and bloggers to reprint with your permission. Make sure to add a "bio box" at the end of your article. Your "bio box" includes your name and contact information (e.g., website address) so that readers of the article can easily contact you.

How to get started quickly?
The fastest way to get any article published is to submit it to an online article directory like www.ezinearticles.com. On this site, web searches will find your article, and many will click on the links in your bio box that link back to your website. Also, many website owners and bloggers syndicate articles from EzineArticles; in doing so, they re-publish the article on their website but must keep the bio box and links to your website.

Here are two important notes for using EzineArticles. First, search through the site to see the types of articles others have written about your topic. This will give you new ideas and also alert you to topics that have already been covered too much. Second, more prominent media sources (e.g., magazines, newspapers) want original content. So, if you have a great idea for an article, pitch it to the more prominent media sources first. Since, once you publish it elsewhere (e.g., on EzineArticles), they won't be interested (although you could then pitch them on another article).

Getting your articles printed in media sources is a simple way to get the word out about your company, control the message, and build lots of credibility. And it doesn't take much time.

And one final tip to make this technique even more efficient—don't start by writing the article. Rather, just start by creating an interesting article title. Then pitch the title to newspaper and magazine editors to see if they are interested (simply call them and/or email them). They may say it's perfect as is, or they may suggest something slightly different. Doing it this way saves time and ensures you write an article they'll publish, which will get you great media exposure and new customers.

Boost Accountability and Boost Results

Accountability has been a buzzword in the business world forever. Unfortunately, most of us have a negative association with the word. We often use it as if it means blame and punishment, as in "Who is accountable for this mistake?" So we unconsciously try to avoid it.

The truth is that accountability is unavoidable. In the workplace, everyone is accountable to someone. As an entrepreneur or business owner, you are accountable to your business' success, and to your customers, investors, and employees.

Now, what if being accountable was empowering for you and your employees? Research indicates that rather than a negative force, holding people accountable for their actions and results has very positive effects on morale and performance.

For your employees, an environment of accountability produces vigilant problem-solving, better decision-making, and greater job satisfaction. With an environment of accountability, employees can develop their skills and be their best. It means a higher likelihood of reaching goals, which we all want.

For yourself, accountability is also key. Most of us worked for someone else in the past to whom we were accountable. But when we struck out on our own and became the boss, we lost that. While many entrepreneurs and business owners are able to be accountable to themselves, it's often challenging. And for tasks that take a lot of discipline (e.g., calling 25 prospective investors every day), sometimes more accountability is needed to make sure they get done.

Here are some ways to boost accountability in your company:

- Create accountability standards for yourself. What happens if you don't complete a task? Do you force yourself to stay late to do it? Or are there no immediate consequences? Figure out how to reward yourself for being fully accountable, and likewise give yourself some sort of penalty when you are not.
- Ambiguity is the enemy of accountability; so your first step as manager of your employees is to make sure they have very clearly defined roles, job descriptions, and duties.

- Accountability is an attitude. Look at yourself as the role model. Are you being accountable to your employees, clients, and yourself? You, as the leader, will want to model this attitude, so focus on being accountable in addition to holding others accountable.

- Do you have written expectations of your employees? Starting at the time of hire, if possible, create written expectations and standards of performance for each employee. You cannot expect something from someone who has not had the opportunity to buy into the expectation.

- Do your employees have a working plan—a project timeline, an economic model, etc.? This will help keep them accountable.

- Do your employees have training? You cannot hold someone accountable to something they have not been trained to do!

- Have you created a learning-based environment? Is it okay to make a mistake or say, "I don't know"? Creating a safe environment for mistakes encourages accountability. Employees will be less afraid to share mistakes and other negative feedback with you that can be used to correct the root of the problem. The opposite of this would be a culture of "yes men" (which you clearly don't want).

- Are there real consequences for lack of accountability in your organization? Consequences work best when spelled out before actually needed, in expectations, for example.

- Do your employees have the talent and ability needed for the task? Some people will not have the ability to do the job you are asking them to do, regardless of having a well-defined role, a great manager, and excellent training. Try to find this out when hiring, but keep an eye on employees throughout their working time with you to confirm it.

Without accountability, no one knows the goal or who is supposed to do what. There's no way of knowing what's going on, so things don't get done (surprise, surprise). Without the right accountability, you will create an environment of low productivity and high turnover.

Conversely, setting up the right accountability structures, as discussed above, will create a culture in which goals are constantly attained.

So make a plan today to implement the tips above. After all, if you don't emphasize and demonstrate the importance of reaching the goals you set, who will?

EPILOGUE

A Balanced Work and Personal Life

"Doubt, of whatever kind, can be ended by action alone." *~Thomas Carlyle*

Isn't it funny how doing less can sometimes be the best way to get a handle on things? Maintaining a healthy life balance is vital; not only for your health and overall well-being, but also for increased productivity in your growing business! If you're a balanced person, you are very likely to achieve your long-term goals. Because the odds are, you're going to run into both ups and downs over time. That's business.

So what would a balanced life look like for an entrepreneur? Can you recognize when one is or isn't? How can we have a balanced life when our schedules are so overwhelming?

Fortunately, there are some tips that will help you regain balance and control of your life. When you will see the first results, you will be a lot more motivated to work hard (when it's time to work), and play hard during the time you choose to reserve for that vital part of living. The secret lies in changing one thing at a time; you need to make small adjustments in order to see what works for you and what doesn't. Slowly but surely, you will get a brand new set of positive and healthy habits!

Here are simple yet effective ideas that will help you:

1. The weekend is all yours!

As soon as Friday evening comes, simply get away from everything that bothers or stresses you. I've heard all sorts of excuses—I know it's hard, trust me, but try to do it completely at least one day per week. You will be amazed to see how good you will feel without the hustle and bustle of projects and to-do's. Spend some time with your close friends and family: a nice dinner, TV/movies, and even some board games will help you relax after a tense week at work! You know it will be waiting for you Monday, so why not tackle it in a relaxed state of mind after a period of rest? (Note: if your business operates on weekends, figure out your slowest day and at least take that one day off; you need time off!)

2. Make a selection.

Write a list and get rid of everything you do not need or that does not add value to your business or life anymore. Simply eliminate everything that has become a stress factor for you and is no longer worth the investment...no mercy!

3. Don't neglect your health!
Everybody knows that it is better to prevent than to treat, so make sure you pay attention to your health. Stress can have devastating effects on both your physical and mental health, and that reflects on your life. Eat healthier, sleep more than you used to, and do some kind of fun, physical activity regularly. Your customers and clients will see the difference in no time!

Importantly, put your health into your routine. For me, many days before or after work I head straight to the gym for a swim and an indoor bike ride. On the bike I have ear phones on, music filling my brain, pushing out everything else. Because this is part of my routine it's easy to do, and I always look forward to it.

4. Get rid of toxins.
The term "toxins" refers not only to what we eat or breathe, but also to those toxic people that surround us. Keep an open mind and gather positive, cheerful people around you. Their positive energy is addictive! This also includes avoiding toxic people; not always easy, but it has to be done.

5. Spend some time alone.
You have a busy schedule like I do, so you certainly know how difficult it is to spend some time on your own. As difficult as it may be, spending some time alone is of utmost importance—it not only relieves stress, but it also encourages creativity! Do something relaxing, something you enjoy doing. You deserve some time for yourself.

6. Strengthen connections with friends and family.
They are the most important people in your life and they deserve a place in your busy schedule. Talk to your friends and family, invite them over for dinner, have a cup of coffee with them. Your loved ones are the constants throughout the fast changes of your life.

No successful person has ever told me they wish they had spent less time with their friends and family during their careers. Rather, it's the opposite, they all wished they had spent *more* time.

7. Treat yourself! You are important; never forget that.

Get a new haircut, buy a new shirt, get your nails done, schedule a massage, or go shopping! Isn't that why we got into business in the first place...to have some perks here and there? Being dedicated to your business doesn't mean being austere. Being dedicated to your own well-being, however, will absolutely help you perform at work.

8. Expand your horizons.

Leaders make better decisions when they have knowledge in a variety of fields and topics. Try to know more about the world that surrounds you-take a stroll in the park, visit a new town or country, attend a local performance, read or watch something outside of your norms. Try something you haven't done before!

9. Last but not least, remember to laugh.

Laugh as loud as you can! Have fun, play or learn new jokes and you will see how beautiful life really is! Being a successful entrepreneur is a long and hard journey; you need to laugh and have fun along the journey!

www.ingramcontent.com/pod-product-compliance
Lightning Source LLC
Chambersburg PA
CBHW051323170526
45166CB00002B/658